YOU HAVE SPIRITUAL GIFTS

AND IT'S TIME YOU USE THEM

VINCE ARNONE

FOREWORD BY
JEFF LEAKE

First Edition

Designed by Matthew Lauletta | harbinger.design
Edited by Elizabeth Lauletta

Printed by Bookbaby

ISBN 9781667814117
Ebook ISBN 9781667814124

I dedicate this to all my teachers, (especially) The Holy Spirit, and to My wife and daughters. I love you.

Also to my parents, my friends, all of the apostles, prophets, pastors, teachers, and evangelists under which I have sat and served, and to all those who have served with me in God's Kingdom.

In all of your life classes, I know there have been many days where I was the troublemaker in the back row who just didn't seem to get it, but I've always been listening, and my experience proves your lessons.

Thank you all, from the bottom of my heart.

CONTENTS

FOREWORD

One of Mark Twain's famous quotes talks about discovering our purpose: "The two most important days of your life are 1) the day you were born and 2) the day you find out why!"

In this book, You Have Spiritual Gifts, Vince Arnone unpacks the foundation of how we begin to understand the why behind our lives. One of the ways we discover our purpose in life is when we start to see what God has put into our lives. There is a deposit of grace that has been given to each person alive. That grace does not just show up in our unique personality, or in the talents and strengths that come through our physically created DNA.

But when a person comes to Christ, there is an additional deposit of God's grace that is imparted into your life. Understanding what that is and how it should work itself out in our lives can, at times, be confusing and even intimidating. I can think back to many times in my pastoral ministry when I was recruiting someone to serve in a ministry role within our congregation. One of the biggest barriers to being used by God is self-doubt. 'How can God use me? I know me!' is often the thought process we have.

What Vince Arnone does in this book is very simply and practically walks us through an understanding of what Spiritual Gifts are and how God begins to use you through them. I think what helps is when we start to comprehend the strategy of God in distributing these gifts throughout the body. When you understand the general definitions and ingenious design of God's gifting to us, you start to see how His practical purposes make sense.

When you see how a hammer is designed, you can see how it makes sense that it should pound nails. When you see the purpose of a level, you can see how essential it is to making sure the foundation is plumb and ready to stand.

It's also true with you. When you see what God made

you to do and be, you can see how God strategically has designs on your life and usefulness. When you do understand and step into that purpose, it is revolutionary. You feel alive. You feel essential. You start to see the results of your life and ministry. And maybe the best of all, you start to experience partnership with Almighty God in bringing about His Kingdom to bear on the earth.

What an honor it is to be a partner with God! To know that you are designed by God with purpose. To understand that you have gifts in your life. This book, You Have Spiritual Gifts, will help you begin your journey toward that end.

Maybe the best part of this book is how it is laid out. The chapters are brief and to the point. The concept of each chapter is clear. It is easy to understand and apply. You actually could read this book as a daily devotional guide. Read a chapter a day, and seek to apply what it describes to you throughout your day. One dose of revelation at a time about who God is, who you are, and how you work together will slowly start to transform your life.

You won't regret taking this journey. You Have Spiritual Gifts is a tremendous way to stride forward into living life to the fullest as you begin to be used by God.

Jeff Leake
Lead Pastor, Allison Park Church
Author: Power For Life, Why Every Believer Needs To Be Baptized In The Holy Spirit

INTRODUCTION

"When my bones were being formed, carefully put together in my mother's womb, when I was growing there in secret, you knew that I was there— you saw me before I was born. The days allotted to me had all been recorded in your book, before any of them ever began."

Psalm 139:15-16, The Good News Translation

WOOOOOOOOOOOOOOOOHOOOOOOOOOOOOOO!

You just made a GREAT decision for the Kingdom of God, for yourself, and for future generations by picking up this book! I can't contain my excitement when I consider the power, the glory of God, and the joy that might overflow in the body of Christ because of this simple act on your part. Those proverbial butterfly wings have started to flap, and a tidal wave is just as surely forming somewhere due to your simple obedience.

Let me explain from where my deep joy for you originates: One of the greatest quests of all human beings is to understand who we are. It is from this most basic question that we begin to learn about the world around us. The initial information we are taught and retain is the first step in our life-long quest to understand how we fit, and the part we play in this world.

In our youngest days, we begin with what we see or what we are told. We know our name. We know our gender. We know our race. We likely know a little something about our ethnicity. Spiritually speaking, if our family goes to church, we know our denomination or lack thereof. We know if we are part of a God-believing family. And if we aren't - we know that, too.

Vince. Boy. White. Italian-American. Roman Catholic family. Those were among my first and most basic steps.

Eventually, all of us innately desire to have a greater understanding of both what we have been told, as well as what we see and observe for ourselves. When we are children, we assume this new knowledge will be just as easy to obtain. There is a voice suggesting to us that there is more. We begin to hope we won't merely find Platonic answers where we are concerned. Instead, we seek a full, significant relationship to the people and dimensions of it all - especially the spiritual and eternal. At this point, while we are still very young, no one has any intention of slowing down in the pursuit of these answers about our deeper identity and purpose for our lives.

As we mature, these suggestions become stronger and more relentless. All of us are forced to make a decision about whether or not we will continue listening to this voice that has been guiding us on this journey to our destiny. Sadly, most people stop somewhere along the line...

- Some people stop before faith in God even steps in. They choose to end with "non-believer" or "atheist" or "agnostic." These individuals, regardless of their education or life experience, cease knowing little more than the basics of their childhood plus (maybe) their profession, and their tastes/likes/dislikes/opinions heaped by whatever shallow terms society decides to place upon them.
- Others choose faith in an impersonal, distant, strange, immoral, or judgmental god or gods that give them little more than an additional moniker accompanied with empty habits. They may be told more about their identity, but they no longer experience it for themselves.
- Some of us come to faith in Christ and discover the true, first and foremost, most beautiful description of who we really are and will always be, even after our earthly bodies and families have long since passed: A son or daughter of God.

This is knowledge that is very, very much worth celebrating!

Alas, many who meet Jesus also just choose to stop and rest there. Some may find the circumstances of life overwhelming and allow themselves to become satisfied with coping rather than overcoming. Others may stop because they've been lied to by God's enemy through the voices and actions of those who have abused or betrayed them. These people might not want to search for more about themselves because they've been taught to fear what they will find. Still others might simply be complacent. They are content to stop at salvation so they can cleanly compartmentalize the "religious" part of their lives, then it doesn't conflict with the time and effort they would prefer to put into other pursuits. For each of these, the voice is still calling out to them to continue the journey - but, sadly, they've stopped responding.

God's call for us continues beyond His saving grace and adoption, and His nudging to discern our identity within Him never stops. One of the most human of human qualities God has ingrained within us is that we will learn about God and who He created us to be - and that we will do so eternally. It is this "double major" that transforms us to be more like Him; for the thoughts He has about us are, after all, His thoughts. When He reveals His creation within us, we get much greater clarity of what we are supposed to do and all the ways in which our paradigms, beliefs, and character must be transformed to be more like what He intended.

An important - and my experience would testify even crucial - portion of the curricula God uses to advance our spiritual development is spiritual gifts. When we learn about the nature of the gifts themselves, it speaks loudly to the power of God as well as the types of things He really values. When we learn about the specific gifts He has chosen to bless us with, it speaks just as loudly to what He values within us as it does to the plans and promises He has for our life. For instance, the gift of healing teaches me that God is very concerned about restoration and wholeness; not just from a salvation standpoint, but the very existence of such a gift means He wants to affect physical restoration and alleviate suffering in this world. If He were to bless me with such a gift, it would suggest my purpose or calling is to serve people who are, indeed, suffering and in need of restoration. It would also indicate a promise in my life: that I will be used to bring Him glory in this way.

Furthermore, the experience of those who act in faith on the gifts He has given them reinforces and develops their identity each and every time they do so. These people are much less likely to ever stop listening to the voice or give up on their eternal journey of learning about God.

And this is why I wrote this book. It's really a systematic collection of biblical knowledge and experiential wisdom from study, living with the Holy Spirit, and from all those who have led me to this point. My hope is that it encourages you to discover both who you are in God, and the promises He has for you. I also pray it exhorts you to keep going until every one of them is fully seized and complete.

At least, that's the meta-physical reason God called me to write it. The real world impetus for the book was actually quite practical, and born out of a bit of frustration. You see, over the last three decades of ministry and church leadership, I have taken dozens of different spiritual gift assessments. Honestly, I've never really liked any of them. I mean, I was glad for them - they did help point me in the right direction from time to time. However, they more often either left me confused about certain things, or they seemed too simplistic to really pinpoint anything significant. They often seemed to lack even a minimal understanding of what the spiritual gifts look like in practice.

For instance, one spiritual gifts test from a prominent mega-church I was researching had an example of, "I tell you the truth regardless of how it affects your feelings." This, according to them, was a way to indicate the gift of prophecy! You know, that spiritual gift Paul says is to, "encourage, comfort, and edify?" I'm sorry, but I think if a person strongly relates to that statement it doesn't make them prophetic - it makes them a jerk! I began to think that if I ever had the opportunity, I would like to create my own assessment. Eventually, my home church, Allison Park Church, asked me to collaborate on an assessment with some of the other pastors, and that process refined much of my thinking.

Soon after, my Lead Pastor, Jeff Leake (a man who sparks the greatest amount of gratitude within my heart of any under which I have ever served) asked me to teach a class on spiritual gifts for the Allison Park Leadership Academy, the school of ministry at our church. The class had been taught in the past, but when I sat down to grab the lesson plans, I discovered that all of the material had been lost! So, I had to create the curriculum from scratch. It is the concepts from this class, along with some of my stories, anecdotes, and research compiled over the last several years that have been structured into this book.

PRACTICAL NOTES

- You can read this book on your own, for sure, but the biblical emphasis of spiritual gifts is to learn how to use them, especially in conjunction with others. I've placed questions at the end of some chapters, which can be utilized for deeper thought or as discussion for a small group.
- This book is deep in some ways, but is also a simple introductory overview or foundational book in others. I've tried to keep it insightful but also light and fun, as I believe these are key qualities of the Holy Spirit, Himself. (Warning, my wife and daughters will tell you expressly that my sense of humor is not for everyone...or maybe anyone. Bottom line, if you don't find it funny - they want me to make sure you know it's definitely not you.)

Anyway - do you hear that?....

His voice is calling again.…

...Your journey continues.

Have fun!!

CHAPTER 1
YOU HAVE SPIRITUAL GIFTS

"I got plenty in my pocket if you're ever in need."

Lukas Graham, "Share that love"[1]

YOU have spiritual gifts.

It's not, "you might" have spiritual gifts.
It's not, "many people" have spiritual gifts (meaning you might not).
It's not, "you are gift-ed" (meaning you're merely naturally talented in some way).

No.

I have never met you, yet, I absolutely know that God has given - or will give you - a spiritual gift, and likely more than one.

These gifts you have been given are unquestionably supernatural. They are not, as so many falsely suppose (and at times teach), simply slightly enhanced personal skills or interests that you have spent a great deal of time, effort, or education practicing. The gifts that God has given to you can be taught about, but they cannot be taught into existence. Either you have been given them or you haven't, and, as I said before…you have been.

You may be reading this book for one or more these reasons:

- You want to know more about the subject of spiritual gifts
- You want to have a deeper definition of specific gifts
- Your friends are a part of one of "those" churches and you just want to understand what they believe without getting into an awkward conversation
- You were assigned or recommended to do so by someone else (oof! I promise to keep it interesting!)
- You have doubts about these phenomena because some-one confidently warned you about perspectives like this, but you've always been curious about the theology

Well, I hate to disappoint you, but while some of

these things may happen as you read these pages, what we will ultimately be doing is identifying YOUR spiritual gifts. However, we'll do it in a way that fills you with understanding, inspiration, and (yes) lots of biblical knowledge that will enable you to impact the people around you in greater ways than you might have ever thought before.

To that end, we're going to embark on this journey like a hike up the Appalachian Trail. We'll start with some detailed briefings about the fundamentals of who the Holy Spirit is, so we have a masterful understanding of where these gifts come from, as well as their purpose. We'll continue into the undulating foothills of prayerful discovery with God and discern the specific gifts you have been given. Once past here, we'll venture into the high peaks of what might be very new territory for you. There, you'll discover your specific calling and the power that God dreams of manifesting through you for His glory. Finally, we'll make our way back down to base camp, reflecting on all we've seen and learned - excited for the next and even greater venture.

Let's begin.

CHAPTER 2

FUNDAMENTAL 1: THE HOLY SPIRIT IS A PERSON

"Pittsburgh third baseman Ke'Bryan Hayes launched a ball down the right-field line that carried over the wall for a home run in Tuesday's game against the Dodgers. Or, rather, what should have been a home run. On video review, it was found that Hayes missed the first base bag when he was rounding the bases."

The Sporting News (June 9th, 2021)[2]

Perhaps one of the most iconic scenes in the history of film is when Daniel Larusso absolutely loses his mind on screen, yelling (and even cussing!) at Mr. Miyogi, the mild mannered and somewhat mysterious building superintendent of Daniel's apartment building. As I'm sure most of you will recall from the 1984 classic *The Karate Kid*, Daniel is an emotional wreck after having been forced to move from New Jersey to California. He's now frustrated because he thought he had convinced Mr. Myogi to teach him karate. Daniel was desperate to defend himself against bullies (who were adept in martial arts) that had been targeting him in his new hometown. He had caught the interest of a girl that used to date their ring leader, and they were not happy about it. Instead, Daniel is commanded to paint walls and fences and sand floors for weeks (all right - I'm not exactly sure how many days had passed - but that's the amount of time the classic 80's rock musical montage seemed to convey). Anyway, sore and tired on a late night, Daniel sees Mr. Myogi casually sauntering home with a fishing pole and a bucket.

We all know what happens next...Daniel throws down the sanding blocks and other tools and tells Mr. Myogi he is through being his own personal slave! As the rant reaches its squeaky (and slightly vile) teen-aged pitch, Mr. Myogi starts barking even more commands, like, "Side! Side!" and "Pain dee fence!" as he throws a series of punches and kicks directly at his pupil. Instinctively and nervously, Daniel deflects every attack with what is no longer merely head-knowledge, but strong, deliberate motion memory now ingrained in his muscles based on the "exercises" his sensei had him working on without his even realizing it.

I still remember my racing heartbeat and sweaty palms watching this scene. Okay, actually, most of this was caused by the fact that I was holding hands with Paula. She was my first girlfriend, and I was on my very first movie date. But, it was also specifically because of this that I was able to so closely relate to the scrawny Italian kid up on that screen, who so wanted to impress his girl! Anyway, back to the scene...

"Hai! Hai! Hai!"..."San de floor!"..."Hai! Hai!"...Daniel is able to block every punch and kick. The dawning spreads across his face as he realizes Mr. Myogi had taught him the fundamentals - and taught him well. The bullies and their dojo may have some fancy skills, but Daniel now has a shot at beating them because he has excellent, foundational karate.

Many times, we can become so determined to assess our spiritual gifts that we don't take the time to learn the fundamentals first. The truth is, without a firm understanding of these basics, the gifts themselves may not be sustained or put to the best use. In fact, scripture teaches us that one of these fundamentals is so important that without ingrained recognition of its supremacy in our thoughts and motivations, the gifts themselves will be completely useless and unfruitful. Understand, the next chapter or two might seem a little basic, or even redundant depending on the extent of your faith walk, but I promise these are simply the "san dee floor!" of your journey into spiritual gifts.

FUNDAMENTAL 1- THE HOLY SPIRIT IS A PERSON

I have several cabinets in my garage to organize my tools. Many of these have shelves and drawers, and I have gone so far as to label and categorize every one. (Yes, I know - I'm one of those guys.) I detest looking for stuff when there's a job to do! I also hate re-purchasing things I know I already have, simply because I can't find where it is. (And you just know, the very second I am done using the newly re-purchased tool, the old one will magically appear!) It took me a lot of effort and expense to get everything just the way I want it so I can always know where every 'whatsamajigger' and 'whozits' is at the very moment I need it.

There's one small two-door cabinet in the middle of my workbench that has three big, painted wooden letters on it spelling "D-A-D." Inside is every letter and note my youngest daughter, Galilee, has ever written to me in her life; so many that it can hardly close. My oldest daughter, Isabella, put the cabinet together for me (with a little help from mom) when she was 8 years old.

Now, if the garage catches on fire while I'm in it, which cabinet and contents do you think I'm grabbing on my way out? Of course, I'm grabbing Isabella's cabinet with all of Galilee's letters! Even though there are many cabinets (and it took greater effort and more money to acquire the contents of the other cabinets - and some of the tools contained within them were, themselves, gifts from people who love me) I am most attached to my daughter's cabinet because it represents a very precious "who" to me, and not just a manufactured "what."

In the same way, in order for us to appreciate, receive and best utilize spiritual gifts, we must understand who we are accepting the gifts from. Many times, we are taught about the Holy Spirit simply by analyzing what He does. We'll get to that, but first let's look at scriptures that teach us about who He is.

Paul conveys this understanding succinctly as he signs off his final letter to the Corinthians: *"The grace of the Lord Jesus Christ, and the love of God, and the fellowship of the Holy Spirit be with you all."* 2 Cor 13:14 (emphasis added). The word "fellowship" in the Greek is "Koinonos", which is also translated elsewhere with terms like "communication", "contribution", and "communion". It would be tremendously difficult to have this type of "fellowship" with an inanimate thing or impersonal being.

The Bible further reveals that this quality of the Holy Spirit's being isn't understood as some sort of theological concept like "personhood." It goes on to describe Him in too many places with traits and tendencies that relate too much to our own humanity for us to think about Him in such a stoic manner. Let me explain with just a few examples:

THE SPIRIT FEELS EMOTIONS:

- GRIEF

"But they rebelled and grieved His Holy Spirit; Therefore, He turned Himself to become their enemy, He fought against them." Isaiah 63:10

"And do not grieve the Holy Spirit of God, by whom you were sealed for the day of redemption." Ephesians 4:30

- LOVE

"Now I urge you, brethren, by our Lord Jesus Christ and by the love of the Spirit, to strive together with me in your prayers to God for me." Romans 15:30

THE HOLY SPIRIT ALSO:

- HAS A MIND

"And He who searches the hearts knows what the mind of the Spirit is, because He intercedes for the saints according to the will of God." Romans 8:27

- SPEAKS

"And the Spirit said to Philip, 'Go up and join this chariot.'" Acts 8:29

(He also speaks in Acts 10:19; Acts 11:12; Acts 13:2; Acts

21:11; Acts 28:25-26; 1 Tim 4:1; Hebrews 3:7-8; Revelation 2:7; Revelation 14:13; Revelation 22:17)

- KNOWS
"For who among men knows the thoughts of a man except the spirit of the man, which is in him? Even so the thoughts of God no one knows except the Spirit of God." 1 Corinthians 2:11

- CAN BE LIED TO
"But Peter said, 'Ananias, why has Satan filled your heart to lie to the Holy Spirit, and to keep back some of the price of the land?'" Acts 5:3

- CAN BE A WITNESS
"And we are witnesses of these things; and so is the Holy Spirit, whom God has given to those who obey Him." Acts 5:32

- CAN BE RESISTED
"You men who are stiff-necked and uncircumcised in heart and ears are always resisting the Holy Spirit." Acts 7:51

It's important when interacting with the Holy Spirit to remember that we are made in His image. The qualities that Jesus displayed when here on earth did not originate when He arrived here, nor were they exclusive to His personhood of God. These same qualities that we see within us, and within Jesus, are shared by the Holy Spirit as well. In other words, the Holy Spirit is not some detached, impersonal entity or powerful force. To believe this is to be closer to practicing zen Buddhism than it is to Christianity, which is based on our relationship with God.

Furthermore, qualities like those above did not originate with us but with God - remember we were made in

His image not the other way around. Therefore, His ability to love, grieve, think, speak, and testify are perfect and reliable, unswayed by circumstance or mood. This is great news! While we can never perfectly know His thoughts, when we approach the Holy Spirit we can begin to develop a familiarity as we would with any other person. Not every question needs to be asked repeatedly because we can come to know and understand what He will say or how He is affected by various words and actions - just like any other person we relate to. In other words, we should often be saying to ourselves, "Well, you already know what the Holy Spirit would say to that" just as easily as we would say, "I know what Dad (or Mom, or my best friend or whoever) might say." His relatable traits make Him intimately know-able.

HOWEVER...
(I did that deliberately because it's a very big "however".)

The love, fellowship, and familiarity we can obtain with the Holy Spirit does not make Him like our "best buddy". He is, definitively, our authority. Pastor and theologian, Richard Pratt, teaches about studying God's word as an "authority dialogue". In other words, we interact with the Holy Spirit and ask for help with our understanding in the same way we would seek clarity from a boss, a parental figure we respect, a coach, etc. He's not our "chum" - He is our "chief". The person who fully walks with the Holy Spirit as a consistent part of their life, and is accessing their spiritual gifts, applies this same principle to all interactions and prayers - not just their study of scripture.

When we consider the Holy Spirit as our God, we don't:
- Avoid or ignore Him like He's just too mysterious and strange to talk to directly.

- Become complacent in our efforts to honor Him, or stop listening intently to what He says. It's actually much the opposite. We listen with an anticipation that each word may be among the most important we will ever hear.

HOWEVER...
(And I did that deliberately because it's big but not really as big as the previous "however".)

The Holy Spirit is still a powerful force. He is a force that brings the Presence of God. This forceful presence is called the "Ruakh" (Roo-ok) in Hebrew. In all of scripture, this name or any derivative is only used to describe the Holy Spirit.

The reason I said this "however" is not as big as the previous one, is that it is only by relating to the Holy Spirit as both a person and an absolute authority that we can begin to consider the Holy Spirit as a force. Call it a product of growing up in the generations of *Star Wars*, but I think it is important to be careful. The Holy Spirit and His gifts are not to be thought of as tools we can hold and manipulate in an effort to master it like a "Jedi" would through various practice and exercise.

As followers of Christ, we are not trying to be a "master" at all. In fact, quite the opposite. If anything, we are to be like a "Jedi Submitter". As it regards the Holy Spirit, any portion of power we sense is based on how well we know Him, how humbly we approach Him, and how thoroughly we invite Him to use us for His end and purposes only. Rather than inflating our egos or helping us in personal gain, seasoned experience teaches the process can inconvenience and even temporarily drain us as God pours us out for others.

Even so, if your attitude and approach are submitted

to Him, you will grow in confidence within the supernatural. Every time He uses you or you witness another being used by the Spirit, you will experience intimacy with God, awe at His power, and joy at His miraculous love for His children in a way that many Christians never witness.

Before we move on to the next fundamental, I wanted to make sure I say a word about the "Trinity":

The Trinity is the name our monotheistic faith gives to our God. It is God, the Father; God, the Son; and God, The Holy Spirit. While separate in personhood, they are one in mind, purpose, substance, and power. The Father is not the Son who is not the Spirit - but they are all, though separate, one God.

If you've been around Christianity for any length of time, you have likely heard about this concept many times. You may have even heard many analogies to describe or explain this "Triune God" we worship.

This may have included an egg: The shell is not the yolk which is not the white. These are separate and distinct but altogether, they are one egg. Without each other, they are not an egg.

Or the sun: The sphere of gas is not the light which is not heat. They are separate, but all together, they make what we know as the sun. Without any one of these three, we would not identify the sun as itself.

The list can go on, but there are two things I want to make clear:

1. It is extremely important that the Holy Spirit who gives you gifts is not a separate entity to be worshiped in a separate format or method from either the Father or Son. They are all one.

2. Because of this, followers of Christ who believe in spiritual gifts can attain at least some unity of mission, and labor and work with those who do not. We worship and serve the same God.

FOOD FOR THOUGHT

- Have you ever spent time worshiping the Holy Spirit? Do you call Him by name during worship and call out to Him?
- When you think about the Holy Spirit, what images come to mind? How do you perceive His character as a person of God? In what ways would you expect Him to interact with you?
- If you were to cast a famous actor or actress in a movie role of the Holy Spirit, who would it be and why?
- Were you ever taught, or have you observed, other analogies of the Trinity besides the ones mentioned in this chapter? (egg/sun) What were they?
- Take a moment, quiet yourself, and pray to the Holy Spirit something like: "Holy Spirit - I pray You reveal Yourself to me in a new way. Teach me not only Your ways but also who You are. As I humbly submit myself to Your will and Your words, encourage me to study You and know You so intimately that I not only hear Your thoughts, but anticipate them like I would any person I deeply admire, respect, and honor. Amen."

CHAPTER 3

FUNDAMENTAL 2: KNOW YOUR ROOTS

"I think of how, perhaps, the best way to fly would be with hands full of earth, so you always remember where you came from."

Ally Condie, 'Matched'[3]

In 2019, ancestry.com reported earnings of $619.6 million from subscription fees alone, which does not include revenues from advertising on its site, which likely exceeds that total. In fact, in August of 2020 a company named "Blackstone" acquired ancestry.com for $4.7 billion! Suffice it to say, people really, really enjoy learning about all the places they are from, and who came before them. Personally, I'm a thoroughbred. One hundred percent Italian on both sides of my family. Three generations removed from immigration on my father's side and two on my mother's. All marriages during that time were also to people of purely Italian descent as well.

One of my favorite memories from when I was young was helping my mother and grandmother make various Italian dishes. One such delicacy was "struffoli pignolata." These were small, honey covered, fried Italian treats served traditionally at Christmas. While we were rolling and shaping the little balls, bow-ties, and rosettes of pastry, they would share stories (that sometimes sounded more like fables or tall tales) of my ancestors.

For instance, my grandfather was a "gaucho" (a cowboy) in Bari, Italy. As a 10-year-old boy, he was already taming horses with his five brothers on a ranch. When his family fled to America - in part, due to the political direction of their home country - he found a job delivering large blocks of ice for people's ice-boxes with a horse-drawn cart to the tenements of New York City. These blocks were very heavy, and the apartment buildings were several stories tall with no elevators. The legend passed on to me as I fried (and snuck a few) of the little dough balls was that my grandfather became immensely, physically strong as a result of this labor. During this time he and my grandmother were courting, and they were on a double-date with their friend who owned an early model motor car, (perhaps a model T or similar) one with the spare mounted on the fender. The story went that they got a flat tire, and they had no jack, so my grandfather lifted the car up himself and held it while his friend changed the tire!

In another tale, my grandfather had started his own business as a butcher and opened a groceria. One day, he and Grandma opened their business in the morning and discovered it was in the process of being robbed by two young men. My grandfather grabbed the two perps by the backs of their necks, bent them over a table, and physically held them with their foreheads pressed against each other while my grandmother called the police!

Like I said, I don't know how much of these stories might have been exaggerated - but a little exaggeration, itself, could be considered a trait of Italian legacy as well! Regardless, these stories filled me with a sense of the sacrifice and determination of the generations that came before me. The Italian phrases sprinkled in here and there as the scenes were described authenticated the sense of history and caused the foods we were making to be more than ingredients, but elements of a robust and lively, individual heritage. It was a beautiful celebration of the fruits of the sacrifice and dreams of people who left their homes to give all of us a new, free life in America. There were so many stories, and many were dramatic and interesting; detailed enough to write another book! It's hard to explain, but even though I've never been to Italy, and we moved from New York when I was 2 years old, the width and breadth of these words somehow grounded me in who I was, and gave me a certain historic identity.

Maybe your family wasn't like mine, and you never really had people sharing legacy stories tied to your ancestry or ethnic heritage. Sadly, many African Americans I know have a permanent detachment from their true cultural heritage, due to the horrors of slavery. But the good news is all of us in the Church - no matter our ethnic heritage - share common stories of our "roots!"

Every one of us who is a part of the Church has tales of historic identity in the Bible. Reading, sharing, and studying them can do a tremendous job of grounding our faith and purpose well beyond that of my childhood culinary exchanges. Best yet, these stories are incredible and immensely intriguing, but free from any exaggeration whatsoever. We've talked about who the Holy Spirit is, but our shared family history is about when He came into the picture. Let's talk a little about when our heritage of spiritual gifts came to be - let's look at Pentecost.

First, let's do some "wax on, wax off." Here are some basic facts that will help you to understand what was going on in the lives of our common family on the day the Holy Spirit was released to our faith-ancestors:

- The Old Testament promise of the day of Pentecost is found in Joel 2:28-29, *"I will pour out my Spirit on all people. Your sons and daughters will prophesy, your old men will dream dreams, your young men will see visions. Even on my servants, both men and women, I will pour out my Spirit in those days."* This promise reveals that everyone is going to receive this gift, regardless of age, or education, or social status, or gender.
- The day is also referred to with much more immediacy by Jesus in Acts 1:4-5, *"Do not leave Jerusalem, but wait for the gift my Father promised, which you have heard me speak about. For John baptized with water, but in a few days you will be baptized with the Holy Spirit."* Incidentally, this is the final command of Jesus on earth - for the apostles to wait for the Spirit before attempting to do anything.
- The scriptural account of Pentecost is found in Acts 2.
- Pentecost literally means "Fiftieth" in Greek.

- Pentecost was also known as the "Feast of Weeks" because it falls seven weeks (or 50 days) after "First Fruits" (or "Passover") which was celebrated with the offering of the first of the barley harvests to God, and the barley harvest took about another seven weeks to fully gather.
- Pentecost, therefore, was seen as a "Harvest Celebration." It was a day of joy and thanksgiving for the end of the barley harvest. However, it also included another first-fruits offering of the wheat harvest, which had only just begun. Wheat was a more significant and larger crop that people depended on to a much greater degree than barley. This beautiful, perfect timing of Pentecost symbolically reinforces the mission of the Holy Spirit through us as stated by Jesus in Luke 10:2, *"The harvest is plentiful, but the workers are few. Ask the Lord of the harvest, therefore, to send out workers into his harvest field."*

The day that God chose to release the Holy Spirit to us happened to be a day that was already celebrated by God's people as the harvest of what had already come - and a promise of a greater yield in the future! In the same way, the Holy Spirit, Himself, is a gift to all of us. What the Spirit enabled His people to do was greater than what could have been conceived of before; certainly greater than anything done in their own strength.

Finally, Pentecost was not simply a day or occasion, but a miraculous empowerment to all of us that continues to this day and on. Every single time the Holy Spirit uses one of us through His gifting it yields both a sort of transformative harvest in the life of the person we are serving, and a promise of a greater harvest to come as the fruit of that moment matures to completion or is shared in testimony as an act of God.

Do you get what I'm saying here? Do you really get it? I have a feeling you don't, so let me state it more plainly:

Just as assuredly as all of your physical traits and characteristics were determined by the people of your physical lineage that came before you, so the spiritual heritage of the specific gifts God has given you can be traced back to that day when the Spirit poured out on Pentecost.

In even plainer words, so I can be really sure you get this:

YOU, YOURSELF, AS GOD MADE AND CRE-ATED YOU, ARE A SPECIFIC PART OF THE HARVEST AND PROMISE OF GOD GIVEN ON PENTECOST. YOUR SPIRITUAL GIFTING IS A NECESSARY COMPONENT IN COMPLETELY FULFILLING THE HARVEST OF OTHER SOULS, ALSO PROMISED ON PENTECOST, THAT YOU ARE DESTINED BY GOD TO WORK!

Your faith and determination to serve God in every way, including with your spiritual gifts, is a result of the harvest of Pentecost - that specific day! You can't read your name in the second chapter of Acts, but you were there! The Ruakh - breath of God that blew the mighty wind that day - is filling your lungs with breath, and is set to empower you in mighty ways this very minute! We all feel a sense of personal history, and maybe even a little obligation to hold up the standards and examples of our biological ancestors. In the same way, we should experience this same desire to supernaturally impact the world around us because of the example set for us by our spiritual ancestors on Pentecost!

Phew! Now THAT was a really great spot for an "Amen!"

Here's what you really need to know: if you read those

last capitalized words in the paragraph above in a "shouting voice" then consider these next words as whispered from your spiritual ancestors: *"You're a big deal. You were precious enough to be bought by Jesus' blood. And you are also a direct descendant of the power poured out on all of us at Pentecost. It's in your spiritual veins. Trust us, what you are about to receive cannot be stopped by any force. on. Earth."*

Yeah. It's so cool...let's just sit here and think about all of that for a moment.

Okay. We're still not ready for an all-out discussion on all of the spiritual gifts. But, let's take a minute and address the first spiritual gift that was poured out on all who believed that day of Pentecost. The gift of tongues.

It's important to note that many things happened on that day. Some of what took place have become known as unique signs of God. These would include the sound of rushing wind, and the tongues of fire. Other signs on that day, however, were *normative*. That is, they could be (and were) repeated many times after Pentecost. They have become a regular occurrence in the body of Christ since that day. The gift of tongues is one of the normative signs, as it continues in our life.

There's been much debate going back centuries over the exact form of tongues that poured out that day. Some believe that what manifested that day were literal other languages, and others maintain it was the "glossa" that Paul refers to in Romans 8:26 when he says, *"...the Spirit helps us in our weakness. We do not know what we ought to pray for, but the Spirit himself intercedes for us through wordless groans ("glossa")."*

In my life, I have experienced the glossolalia (or 'glossa') as many do. But, I have also heard of the literal language from an unwitting individual. Here is one such testimony:

Many years ago, friends of mine, Bernie and Jeanette, led a small group I joined shortly after coming to faith in Jesus. Though he worked professionally as an engineer, and she was in business, they were incredible disciple-makers. Eventually, they began to feel they were called into ministry, and they desired to plant a church overseas. They just didn't know where. After months of prayer and discernment of their own as well as that of our pastors and friends, they still had no idea. They began to have doubts about what God had told them, but they decided to begin to travel around the world to interact with missionaries and brothers and sisters of our church before making a final decision on where to plant a church (or even if they should do so at all).

Eventually, they were on a trip in Indonesia. While there, they were participating in a large prayer meeting with some missionaries who knew them and the call on their heart. They were invited up front for prayer. Everyone began to pray using the gift of tongues. After a few moments, Bernie and Jeanette stopped as they realized the room had gone silent. They opened their eyes, looked out, and saw a room of stunned faces. The prayer leader asked Jeanette if she had ever been to Indonesia before or learned the Indonesian language. She answered, truthfully, that she hadn't done either. People began to laugh as the leader went on to explain that she had just recited - in perfect Indonesian - the Lord's prayer! Pastors Bernie and Jeanette took this as God's sign this was the place of their calling. They eventually planted The Collective Church in Jakarta, which became a large and thriving church that made many new disciples of Christ in this predominantly Muslim country. They oversaw it for more than 20 years.

My perspective is that it is likely both glossa and earthly, but unlearned, language took place on the day of Pentecost. When reading Acts 2, there's actually even a third possibility. The actual scripture that refers to the Jews from many nations hearing what was being said reads: *"When they heard this sound, a crowd came together in bewilderment, because each one heard their own language being spoken."* - Acts 2:6. It doesn't denote whether the actual language was literally spoken, only that those there heard it in their own language. It's possible that God caused them to hear it however He wanted them to, regardless of what was being spoken. I suppose this could also be true for Bernie and Jeanette in the story I shared above.

The bottom line is, I don't know what form the gift of tongues took on that particular day. But, I do know that the gift of tongues was initiated then and continues to this day. It is a promise that was given to all who desire to receive it. Again, here's Acts 1:4-5, when Jesus told us so, prophesying about the day of Pentecost and beyond: *"On one occasion, while he was eating with them, he gave them this command: 'Do not leave Jerusalem, but wait for the gift my Father promised, which you have heard me speak about. For John baptized with water, but in a few days you will be baptized with the Holy Spirit.'"*

My pastor, Jeff Leake, in his book, Power for Life, (a book I kiddingly refer to as, 'the little Holy Spirit Bible') elaborates on these verses by saying this, "The baptism in the Holy Spirit is a promise that is given to all who show up for it. It isn't something we earn by being worthy. It's something we obtain simply by showing up to receive that which God has promised to give us."[4]

And along with that, it's a big feature of your spiritual

heritage. If you have never received the gift of tongues, I encourage you, right now, to pause and ask the Holy Spirit to fill you so you might do just that. Pray, "Holy Spirit - I ask you to fill me. Jesus, I ask you to baptize me with the Holy Spirit, so I might receive the gift promised to me." Now, whatever comes to mind, whatever syllable crosses your mind, let it come through your lips, and keep going for a bit. If nothing happens, don't worry. There isn't anything wrong with you. I encourage you to share your desire with a friend or pastor that does speak in tongues, so they might pray with you.

Whether you just now received this gift (HALLELU-JAH!!) or it has already been a part of your life - or it hasn't quite yet - there is so, so much to learn. His desire is for you to fully realize not just one, but all of the gifts He has destined to put within your spirit.

But know this, too: the power you have will not ignite…

It will not do its work through you…

If you do not completely embrace the 3rd and most important fundamental in the next chapter.

With it, there is no complacency, or sin, or evil that can withstand your gaze let alone your prayers.

Without it, this book is an empty read and you will harvest…

Nothing.

So, just a little more "wax on, wax off"…go ahead and turn that page.

FOOD FOR THOUGHT

- What is your family's ethnic heritage? Did you have any family cultural things you used to do/foods you used to make/phrases you used to say? If so, what were they? Which was your favorite?

- Whether you know your ancestral heritage or not, how does it make you feel/what thoughts come to mind when you consider your spiritual heritage as a member of the body of Christ (the Church), and its birth at Pentecost? Does this cause you to view the purpose of your life differently? Does this cause you to view the people you go to church with differently?

CHAPTER 4

FUNDAMENTAL 3: THE ULTIMATE PURPOSE OF SPIRITUAL GIFTS

"We thought we had the answers.
It was the questions we had wrong."

U2, "11 o'clock Tick Tock"[5]

Many people think their faith, their actions, and their spiritual gifting are enacted at different times and for completely different purposes. You pray at one time, you serve at another, and utilize a supernatural spiritual gift on yet another occasion all in different places. While this may be logistically true in certain seasons, the reality is they are all intertwined by an absolutely essential, common thread. It's made plain in scripture repeatedly, and in multiple contexts from the very beginning of the Bible until the very end.

Most studies I have seen or read over many years convey the fact that the majority of Americans have a much higher opinion of Jesus than they do the Church. With Jesus having fulfilled His earthly mission, the bride of Christ will now bear the wounds from the whips of the world on behalf of her Savior. But we all know the accusations aren't, by any means, without merit. I believe this fact is caused by the attitudes and misconceptions of some believers that I just highlighted in the previous paragraph.

I propose the only truly empowered church is a church composed of people who have both complete belief in and practice of spiritual gifts on a daily basis and who also fundamentally understand - in the deepest and most personal way - why they do so. Let's look at the passage that may be the most beautiful and accurate depiction of the ministry of spiritual gifts. It's the great big, huge, historical faith-moment found in Luke 10:30-35. In common Christian terms, this is referred to as "The Good Samaritan."

"Jesus replied, 'A man was going down from Jerusalem to Jericho, and fell into the hands of robbers, who stripped him, beat him, and went away, leaving him half dead. Now by chance a priest was going down that road; and when he saw him, he passed by on the other side. So likewise a Levite, when he came to the place and saw him, passed by on the other side. But a Samaritan while traveling came near him; and when he saw him, he was moved with pity. He went to him and bandaged his wounds, having poured oil and wine on them. Then he put him on his own animal, brought him to an inn, and took care of him. The next day he took out two denarii, gave them to the inn-keeper, and said, 'Take care of him; and when I come back, I will repay you whatever more you spend.'"

What a beautiful story.

Here we have the depiction of two religious "church" people: a priest, and then an even more devout man known as a Levite (like a "super priest" descendant of the priestly tribe of the Israelites). Both men choose not to take care of the wounded victim of robbery.

The priest and Levite did precisely what the law and the culture of the time would have expected of them. When they passed by on the other side, this was considered the good and right thing to do. The law forbade those washed for religious offering to touch anything unclean, and a beaten and bloody man lying in a ditch was certainly unclean.

So, in this passage, Jesus is teaching (and prophesy-ing) a better way - a way that He was living in His ministry on earth, and in concert and agreement with the Holy Spirit. The Samaritan not only touches the man, but transports, houses, and pays for all of his needs with great personal and financial sacrifice. This is such a beautiful depiction of the role of both Jesus in salvation, as well as the church, in the way in which Jesus expects us to reach the world. This certainly points us right at the very center of the reason we are each given and expected to use spiritual gifts.

As far as spiritual gifts go, there's a moment that may have been directly prior to this moment that we need to look at. It more plainly reveals the fundamental reason for spiritual gifts in our world. The verses preceding the Good Samaritan in Luke, as well as an account from the 22nd chapter in Matthew, are extremely similar. Scholars agree the "Pharisee expert in the law" in Matthew and the "lawyer" in Luke 10 may very well have been the same person and the record is of the same event. With that hypothesis and a little logic in mind, let's look at how an epic battle of wits may have gone down:

Jesus shared the parable of the Good Samaritan in response to the questions a lawyer had posed to him. He was, most likely, a hired gun of the Jewish religious councils who had been publicly embarrassed by Jesus on the occasions of the woman who was caught in adultery (John 8) and when asked about paying taxes (earlier in Matthew 22). Not wanting to experience such a butt-whooping again, they appointed a spokesperson; someone who would have been known for his acumen for debate.

The lawyer begins to attempt to lay a trap in verse 22:36 when he says, *"Teacher, which is the greatest commandment in the Law?"* He isn't simply trying to get Jesus to identify a particular commandment as superior - he was laying the snare. If Jesus had chosen any one of the ten, the lawyer would have been able to use any one of the other commandments as destructive suppositions. For instance, the lawyer could reply, "How can you say 'I am the Lord your God - you shall not have other Gods before me?' Are you, therefore, saying that so long as I believe in God I can violate the ninth commandment and take my neighbor's wife? Or the seventh and steal from him? Or the eighth and lie to him? Why should I not do all three?" Regardless of whichever one Jesus would have chosen, he likely had an encompassing (and even entertaining) retort based on the remaining 9, and his intent would have been to mock and degrade him. Hence, he would have laid the fencing around his intellectual "House of Pain" where he and Jesus would intellectually "MMA" in the style of match where the best debaters might only hope for a tie.

But this was Jesus. No one traps Him unless He wants them to, and Jesus was not inclined to do so that day. He responds by quoting part of what was known as 'The Shema,' a verse recited during Jewish feasts taken from passages of Deuteronomy and Numbers.) He says in verse 37 & 38:

> "'Love the Lord your God with all your heart and with all your soul and with all your mind.' This is the first and greatest commandment."

If Jesus had stopped there, like we said, the lawyer would have pounced. If he was that skilled, he would have expected the potential of Jesus to dodge. He could liken it to the first of the ten commandments (since it is so similar) and set off on his chain of destructive comebacks about what Jesus left out...but Jesus didn't stop there. Instead, Jesus completely threw off the lawyer's feeble attempts and did something completely unexpected. He added to the chief commandment by quoting another, heretofore, less prominent law (but also found in Leviticus). He does not - in any way - violate or invalidate the law but, rather, expands its scope. In this next moment, He completely changes how the purpose of faith had always been understood; and that change lasts until this very day. He speaks of the reason - the MOST fundamental of the fundamentals for spiritual gifts...the "waxiest" of all the "wax ons, wax offs"...

> "And the second is like it. Love your neighbor as yourself." (Matthew 22:39)

Boom. Repeated moments of silence must have hung in the air…

It must have been such a shock. The lawyer couldn't argue with it. Certainly, "love of neighbor" is the outcome of the totality of the law, but it couldn't have been an assertion he was expecting in response to his question about commandments! Trying to save himself, he stammers out a stupid question:

"And who is my neighbor?" (Luke 10:29)

And that perfectly served up Jesus' most famous parable that we reviewed together a few moments ago - the parable of the Good Samaritan.

By now, you are probably locking onto the most foundational "wax on, wax off" principle of why spiritual gifts exist and what must encapsulate your heart and attitude before you even begin to use them.

Before we crescendo into it, let's look back at a big moment before this great big moment between Jesus and the lawyer because it makes the example Jesus chose in his reply to the lawyer's question even that much more amazing:

"As the time drew near for him to ascend to heaven, Jesus resolutely set out for Jerusalem. He sent messengers ahead to a Samaritan village to prepare for his arrival. But the people of the village did not welcome Jesus because he was on his way to Jerusalem. When James and John saw this, they said to Jesus, 'Lord, should we call down fire from heaven to burn them up?' But Jesus turned and rebuked them. So they went on to another village." (Luke 9:51-55)

All of this is recorded in Luke 9, and is known to have

immediately preceded the events of the lawyer's questioning. Just before this happened, Jesus had sent the disciples out among the people to tell them the "kingdom of God is near." They returned performing many miracles. They were filled with the Holy Spirit that Jesus had imparted to them, and had been performing the same acts that we will be studying (and identifying within you) in the rest of this book: Healing illnesses, casting out demons, cleansing lepers and so on. The fame and reputation of these acts had spread almost as far and as fast as it likely would today. Most were very receptive to this. The news had even reached the evil King Herod, and the influence of the people's enthusiasm had worried him.

However, not everyone was overjoyed by these acts. The people of one particular region rejected all of the kindness and joy and good news of these miracles simply on the basis of Jesus' race. Their ingrown hatred of a man they had never met - even one coming in the very name of peace and love, where they could only stand to gain and not lose - could not overcome a loathing so profound. They wouldn't even allow him to set foot on their land. So obvious was their outward bigotry that it arose the same sort of counter-reaction in Jesus' own disciples. (And He rebuked them for it.) Did you read who these people were? Perhaps you need to go back to the passage again and look at it once more and enjoy the shock yourself.

I'll just wait here for you...

Incredible isn't it? It was Samaria! The region of centuries-old racist hate between themselves and Jews in response to seemingly endless war and depravity. They all had excellent reasons for their hatred. Jesus wanted to go there, specifically, to show His love and break the barriers between them. In response, they completely and utterly rejected Him.

When questioned just a short time later - confronted by the hit-man lawyer intent on destroying His public reputation - Jesus used the Samaritan as the example of true love in his reply. Jesus was willing to utilize the power of the Holy Spirit to serve and love even enemies. Instead of denouncing them when He was rejected by those very people, He first rebukes His own disciples for wanting to avenge the moment, and then even honors and upholds them publicly!

That's true love...and if we don't have that kind of selfless, self-abandoned love in our hearts we will not experience the fullness of spiritual gifts in our life. No matter who comes before you, and no matter who you encounter in your life, you must love them as Jesus loves them first. This must be so before the Holy Spirit can ever work.

You cannot heal for your own glory...

You cannot prophesy for your bank account...

You cannot minister to the needs of others out of mercy and compassion with the expectation of adulation and thanks...

You must lay yourself down and serve others fundamentally and completely in your heart and mind *first*. The power of the Holy Spirit will flow through you just as assuredly as it did for the disciples.

Faith in the goodness of God and His desire to bring His Kingdom on earth is absolutely essential; but love is just as much so. Jesus said so Himself, *"and the second is just like it: love your neighbor as yourself."*

That statement changed the world...

That statement changed your world...

And you must sincerely live by it if you want to change the world in His name and with the power of your spiritual gifts.

In the next chapter, we're going to seek to get this final "wax on, wax off" principle of love down from your head and more into your heart with a simple exercise.

FOOD FOR THOUGHT

- Who is the most loving person you have known? Why do you feel this way about them?
- Using your thoughts about the person who came to mind in the last question, what is your personal definition of love?
- If there was one thing you could do for every person in your church, what would it be?

CHAPTER 5

GOOD LOVIN'...

Love is not love
Which alters when it alteration finds,
Or bends with the remover to remove.
O no, it is an ever-fixed mark
That looks on tempests and is never shaken;
It is the star to every wand'ring bark,
Whose worth's unknown, although his height be taken.

William Shakespeare (Sonnet 116)[6]

Likely the most famous passage of the Bible is 1 Corinthians 13. It's read and spoken the whole world-wide on many occasions, particularly at weddings. Many of those who have these verses as a part of their special day may not even believe in the Bible or God, let alone the actual context in which it is written. It sounds beautiful, but when recognized for what it is and why and when Paul was inspired to write it, its true beauty is properly seen. Potentially, it is the most significant and piercing challenge to those who aspire to live an abundant life, centered on the miraculous activity of the Holy Spirit.

Of course, challenging scriptures aren't meant to condemn or frustrate. They are there, at least in part, for us to personally assess. When James says, *"Consider it pure joy when trials of all sorts befall you,"* it isn't meant to be received as, "Okay. Got it. Move on to the next one." It's stated in its blunt form of exhortation to make us stop and consider, "Do I really consider it joy when bad stuff comes my way in this world?"

One could say the same thing about the fruit of the spirit as listed off by Peter at the top of his letter. It's not just an inventory to be checked off like a grocery store shopping list: "Got love here - yep. Got peace in aisle 2 - and let's swing by aisle three for some joy," etc. As we read it, we're thinking, "Am I loving? Am I joyous? Am I peaceful?," etc.

The same thing applies to 1 Corinthians 13 and its particular elaboration on the Christian love. In context, it is written to a church that had been abusing and misusing spiritual gifts. Paul writes the entire letter with a balance of rejoicing that they, at least, were pursuing the gifts, and had a thirst for increasingly deeper and more intimate knowledge of God. In fact, Paul attributes the volume of gifting they have seen to this very fact. In the first paragraph of his first letter he says, *"Therefore (because you've been so enriched by*

God with all sorts of knowledge) you do not lack any spiritual gift." (1 Corinthians 1:7) He's admitting they literally have it all - the whole package of gifts among them.

By the time he gets along to 13 chapters later, he has just finished pointedly explaining how selfish and chaotic their worship experiences had become as a result of their inappropriate use of spiritual gifts, and he desires to show them "a better way." Now, obviously, the 13th chapter isn't about order of service. It is certainly more personal. Paul is neither mincing words, nor changing the subject. He commandingly explains to us how our personal understanding and practice of true, Godly love will solely determine the effectiveness and impact of spiritual gifts. The first several verses of chapter 13 make the most sense when looked at with this understanding:

> "If I speak in the tongues[a] of men or of angels, but do not have love, I am only a resounding gong or a clanging cymbal. If I have the gift of prophecy and can fathom all mysteries and all knowledge, and if I have a faith that can move mountains, but do not have love, I am nothing. If I give all I possess to the poor and give over my body to hardship that I may boast, but do not have love, I gain nothing."

He isn't just saying, "If I speak all worldly languages like French, Spanish, English, Aramaic, etc…" followed by statements of when to prophesy. He is dramatically emphasizing the most significant ingredient to Godly operation of all spiritual gifts as founded upon the very commandment of Christ we already spoke about: love. It's extremely important to understand chapter 13 is directly and entirely related to chapter 12. It is not a sudden, separate train of thought. He's still 100% speaking about spiritual gifts. He is not saying,

"Put these other silly practices entirely aside and just love people." Nor is he contradicting what he just spent so much time explaining in the previous passages by dismissing them in favor of embodying a certain countenance or demeanor. Much to the contrary, he's emphasizing the core motivation that enables spiritual gifts to become the most potent, and what that motivation looks like in overall personal practice. Spiritual gifts grow out of the love of God bestowed upon us, and it is out of an overflow of this love that we use them in ministry to others. With that in mind, let's look at verses 4-6. Read it slowly. Concentrate. Meditate on each sentence.

"Love is patient, love is kind. It does not envy, it does not boast, it is not proud. It does not dishonor others, it is not self-seeking, it is not easily angered, it keeps no record of wrongs. Love does not delight in evil but rejoices with the truth. It always protects, always trusts, always hopes, always perseveres."

Now, let's do what this passage is really meant to cause us to do - assess. First, pray for your gracious Father to gently speak to you. Then, read these verses again below. But, this time, in each of the blanks, say your own name rather than "love." It can sometimes make it more pointed to do this while reading it out loud:

_____ is patient. _____ is kind. _____ does not envy. _____ does not boast. _____ is not proud. _____ does not dishonor others. _____ is not self-seeking. _____ is not easily angered. _____ keeps no record of wrongs. _____ does not delight in evil but rejoices with the truth. _____ always protects. _____ always trusts. _____ always hopes. _____ always perseveres.

Some simple questions - answer as honestly as you can:
- Do you feel if these statements were made about you, just like you read them, they would be true?
- Which statements were the most difficult for you to say? Which ones caused you to recall some moments you wish you had back?
- In which of these capacities of love do you feel you have the most need to grow?

Chances are, this simple exercise proved to be a bit difficult. The good news is the most abundant gift God, Himself, bestowed upon us through Jesus was grace. There's no condemnation because of what you have discovered. Much the opposite; when we take such things seriously, under God's guidance, it quite pleases Him.

But, it is also true that grace - no matter how powerful and all encompassing - does not change the standard. There lies the true rub. The standard of, "Love your neighbor as yourself" is even farther reaching than the ten commandments. It is this standard of love toward all those who come before us in need of ministry that we must selflessly uphold if we want the kind of access to the spiritual gifts God desires for us.

Many, in error, think using our spiritual gifts is a matter of greater faith. However, again in context, Paul the Apostle of God, ends the passage by reminding it is a matter of love:

"And now these three remain: faith, hope and love. But the greatest of these is love." (1 Corinthians 13:13)

Let me give you one more passage on which to meditate. There's no exercise with this. I will pose no deep, probing questions to you.

I think it's important to remind ourselves of perfect love in action; the most specific depiction of who we are to be when approaching those God brings us; the true standard of love we are to aspire to, lest we practice these gifts and yet still remain "nothing."

One last little thing I ask of you: read Philippians 2 slowly and deliberately with consideration of all Jesus did, was, and is, right in this very moment:

> "Therefore if you have any encouragement from being united with Christ, if any comfort from his love, if any common sharing in the Spirit, if any tenderness and compassion, then make my joy complete by being like-minded, having the same love, being one in spirit and of one mind. Do nothing out of selfish ambition or vain conceit. Rather, in humility value others above yourselves, not looking to your own interests but each of you to the interests of the others. In your relationships with one another, have the same mindset as Christ Jesus: Who, being in very nature God, did not consider equality with God something to be used to his own advantage; rather, he made himself nothing by taking the very nature of a servant, being made in human likeness. And being found in appearance as a man, he humbled himself by becoming obedient to death—even death on a cross!
>
> Therefore God exalted him to the highest place and gave him the name that is above every name, that at the name of Jesus every knee should bow, in heaven and on earth and under the earth, and every tongue acknowledge that Jesus Christ is Lord, to the glory of God the Father."

And now, "Daniel-san"... your basic training is over.

No more "wax on, wax off."

It's time to train up for the tournament we're all a part of.
It's time to reverse and destroy the effects of evil in this world.
It's time to bring heaven on earth.

It's FINALLY time to discover your spiritual gifts.

CHAPTER 6
SPIRITUAL GIFTS
ASSESSMENT

"No one who discovers who God has made him or her to be
would ever want to be anyone else."

Bill Johnson, "The Power That Changes The World"[7]

Before you take the spiritual gifts test, a few clarifying words about the assessment:

As with any spiritual gifts assessment, this is meant to only be an indicator of what God had placed within you. It, in no way, is meant to limit what you believe God can do through you. In fact, any assessment such as this one is limited, in and of itself, to only measuring what God has already given you. There's no way to assess, in written form, what God plans to do.

You may have taken spiritual gifts assessments in the past. You'll likely find that this one will follow the same method as most you've done before. However, there are a couple of aspects of its content that might be slightly unique:

First, I've tried to be very disciplined to include as many of the gifts from Corinthians and Romans as possible. That means this test is meant to help you assess the presence or tendency of the following gifts in your spirit:

Prophecy
Serving
Teaching
Exhortation
Giving
Leadership
Compassion
Word of Wisdom
Word of Knowledge
Faith
Healing
Discernment
Interpretation of Tongues

A few of these gifts such as, "interpretation of tongues," "word of knowledge," and "word of wisdom" are often left off of spiritual gifts assessments. I'm sure the thought process of the author is, "either you have done it or not, and it's hard to make up multiple examples about it for a test." That is certainly logical and, yes, including these was a bit of a challenge. However, I did so for two reasons:

1. I think some of you have already experienced these things. Therefore, I think it's important to assess them alongside your other spiritual gifts. This assessment would miss its intended purpose if it devalued certain gifts you have been given in deference to those that are easier to put on a written exam.

2. I think some of these kinds of "seeing" and "hearing" gifts get lumped into 'prophecy' on some spiritual gifts exams - which they really aren't. This becomes key when you consider that Paul exhorts us all in 1 Corinthians 14 to prophesy as it is the gateway to the release of many of the other spiritual gifts. (We'll discuss this concept more in a couple of chapters). Word of Knowledge and Word of Wisdom are beautiful gifts, but they won't accomplish the same thing as prophecy, and so should remain distinct.

That being said, I did completely exclude the gift of tongues, itself, because I believe it is both available to all and directly associated with baptism in the Holy Spirit, just as we discussed when talking about our common roots in Pentecost. Even if you do not share these specific beliefs with me, I certainly can't figure out how to separate it from the aforementioned, "either you have experienced it or you haven't" perspective. I also eliminated "miraculous powers" (as most do) because as exciting as it sounds, it is completely undefined. There is simply no way to know what it is, specifically.

Finally - and also because I wanted to stay disciplined to the aforementioned scriptural lists - I have also excluded other gifts often placed on these tests. Many of these skills are good and useful, but they aren't on the biblical lists of those gifts that are truly spiritual in nature. Even with the very best intentions, I think us pastors sometimes give in to the pressures of managing what can be a big and wobbly organization of voluntary workers called a church. When there's people to attract and hold, songs to be sung, buildings to be constructed and maintained, money to be managed, etc...We have a tendency to define certain things like leading worship, building stuff, and even, essentially, the talent to host a party as "spiritual gifts". But that isn't in the Bible. Yes, there are examples of people who possess these talents and skills being used by God:

- Craftsmen were gathered to finish the building of the temple
- David and Ezra (among others) gathered the musicians to lead the people in worship
- Priscilla and Aquilla's hospitality enabled Apollos to fully understand "The Way" of Jesus
- Peter preached in such a way that thousands were evangelized to and committed their hearts to Christ

But, according to the Bible, these are not really "spiritual gifts." There may very well be spiritual gifts used in what they did, and we have many examples of biblical figures impacting others through these talents. However, they aren't listed as "spiritual gifts" in the relevant sections of Scripture I cited above.

There is a good reason for this. When I consider it, my own occasional pastoral cheating when amalgamating these gifts and skills in the past may have caused unintentional sluggishness to movements of God. That reason being: Many of these are ministries we are all called to engage in, regardless of how good or blessed or talented we are at them.

Here's what the Bible says regarding some of these examples:

> We are all to continually worship God, not just when accompanied by those of us who can sing or play instruments: *"I will extol the Lord at all times. His praise will ever be on my lips."* - Psalm 34:1

> We are to always be hospitable, not just those of us who are extroverted and cook well: *"Do not forget to be hospitable to everyone, for some have entertained angels without knowing it."* - Hebrews 13:2

> We are all to participate in the great commission by sharing our faith: *"And if someone asks you about your christian hope, always be ready to explain it."* - 1 Peter 3:15

Therefore, my hope is that we will all participate in such activities robustly. I don't want to, in any way, cause anyone to not participate in doing so because I inadvertently convinced you that you must be "gifted" in order to do so.

All right, already! - Let's get on with it!

So here's the instructions:
- Be sure you have 30-45 minutes set aside for this exercise with no distractions.
- For each statement, place a number between 1 and 5 that corresponds with how much you agree or relate to each statement in the blank. A guide for what each number

means is below.

- Answer as honestly as you can. If you haven't ever experienced something or you don't understand it, place a "1" in the blank.

We'll give further instructions on how to score your exam and determine your gifts after you've completed it. Have fun!

1	2	3	4	5
Almost Never	Seldom	Sometimes	Frequently	Almost Always

1. It deeply saddens and even troubles me when people don't know who God has called them to be, or what to do with their life. _____
2. I'm most comfortable doing things "behind the scenes." _____
3. I absolutely love studying the Bible in depth. _____
4. It's extremely important to me that after we talk you leave more uplifted than when we started. _____
5. One of the most important things I regularly do is give money over and above my tithes/offerings to people in need. _____
6. I enjoy managing people, time frames, schedules, etc.. _____
7. I will set aside tasks I need to complete to go see or meet someone who is in need. _____
8. After talking with friends about their problems, they often come back and tell me that what I said made all the difference and helped them figure it out. _____
9. There have been many times that God has told me to pray for someone about something specific they hadn't told me, only to find out later they needed those exact prayers. _____
10. If I'm being totally honest, I sometimes struggle to relate

to those who have doubts about God's power. _____

11. I have often prayed for sick people and they have gotten well much more quickly than anyone expected. _____

12. There have been clear occasions that I have felt the need to pray for God's protection over me even when the people, places, and things around me don't appear immediately dangerous. _____

13. I most often hear God speaking to me when either I or someone with me is speaking in tongues. _____

14. When I pray, I often hear or sense the thoughts of God about myself and others. _____

15. I have often said something like, "Listen, just tell me what to do, and I'll do it. Whatever it is, just let me know." (And if they tell me, I do it.) _____

16. Whenever I hear a great message or my mind gets blown from something I found in my own study of the Bible, I start to think about who else needs to know it, too, and I share it with them as accurately as I can. _____

17. I have a knack for motivating people to sign up/get involved. _____

18. I find ways to increase my income so I can have more available to give. _____

19. I prefer to delegate responsibilities to accomplish tasks. _____

20. I'm emotionally affected when people tell sad stories, even when I don't know them. _____

21. God has often given me useful, specific guidance or wisdom on issues I otherwise know nothing about. _____

22. I can recall times God has given me specific and deliberate factual knowledge about something practical that I have never learned. _____

23. When someone is facing a terminal illness, I will keep praying for total healing no matter what. _____

24. When I sit down to pray for people, I find myself praying

most often for those who are sick or injured. _____

25. I can recall times discussing things with my family or at work where I supported an idea that didn't sound as good as some others simply because I had a sense it was what God wanted. _____

26. Sometimes, when someone is speaking in tongues around me, I feel compelled to pray about something very specific. _____

27. God sometimes gives me an encouraging dream or picture in my mind when I'm praying for someone. I feel the need to share it with that person. _____

28. If I see a helpful task that needs to be done, I feel I need to drop whatever else I am doing and try to do it. _____

29. If I know how to do something and I think it might help you, I will prioritize the time it might take to show you how it's done. _____

30. I love to help others believe in themselves and take on new challenges. _____

31. Having more means I can give more. Period. _____

32. I am passionate about coordinating strategies and what is needed to execute them. _____

33. When others hurt, it makes me hurt, even when it's the result of their own actions. _____

34. When some non-believers question my faith, God often enables me to know exactly how to respond with an accurate and Godly answer. _____

35. I have felt compelled to pray for someone about a specific need they hadn't told me about, and found out later they were dealing with that very problem. _____

36. It comes naturally for me to see God's handiwork even in hard circumstances. _____

37. More than once, I have prayed for someone who was sick and they were immediately healed. _____

38. Sometimes, someone says something and I just absolutely know it is God speaking through them, even if they don't know it at the time. _____

39. I've been around people speaking in tongues, and I swear it's like they are speaking my language. _____

40. Often I am praying for someone and, whether I know them or not, God compels me to share an encouraging statement or brings to mind an uplifting scripture that I just know they need to hear. _____

41. I just have a knack for knowing the kinds of things I can do that help people without being told. _____

42. It saddens me very deeply when I hear or read something about God that I know is not biblically accurate. I take efforts to make sure those I know and care about understand the truth. _____

43. In between my busy-ness, I like to take time to send a note, email, text, etc. just to brighten someone's day for no reason. _____

44. Whenever I am blessed with a sum of money beyond my needs that I did not expect, my first thought is whether God gave it to me to share with someone else. _____

45. While I can do a lot on my own, I prefer to organize a team to get the job done. _____

46. When homeless people hold up signs, I read them. I can't always stop, and it pains me to pass by. _____

47. Often when I pray for someone, God shares with me what they need to specifically do about a problem I know they are facing. _____

48. I have been in prayer for someone I care about, and God has revealed to me a secret problem they are facing, and I knew I was supposed to help them. _____

49. My first response to the biggest challenges is to pray and declare a Godly outcome. _____

50. When I have prayed for people who are physically ailing, they told me the moment I touched them, they already began to feel better. _____
51. I often have the sense of the presence of evil in a person or place, and I am moved to effectively pray for God's protection. _____
52. Nearly all of the times that I recall hearing the voice of God in a public setting took place when someone was speaking in tongues. _____

Now, it's time to score the exam. Fair warning - get ready for just a little page flipping:

1. Transfer your numeric answers into the score sheet below. Be sure to keep your answer for the first statement in blank 1, the second in blank 2, etc.
2. Add across each column and place the totals in the blank under 'total.' For instance, you'll be adding your answers from questions 1, 14, 26, and 40 together and writing the total in the adjacent blank. Then your answers from 2, 15, 27, and 41 together and writing the total in its blank, etc.
3. When you're all through, take note of your highest 3 totals over at least a score of 12. The spiritual gift listed on the far right side and located in those rows are your spiritual gifts.
4. If you have a tie among more than 3, it's fine to consider all of them as what God is depositing in you. If, however, you have a great number of the same total, you might want to take a break, refresh your mind, and come back to take the exam again at another time. If you have no totals higher than 12, just take the highest 3 you have. Circle those in your book, and then move on to the next chapter where we discuss each of the spiritual gifts.

QUESTIONS				TOTAL
Prophecy				
1.	14.	27.	40.	=
Serving				
2.	15.	28.	41.	=
Teaching				
3.	16.	29.	42.	=
Exhortation				
4.	17.	30.	43.	=
Giving				
5.	18.	31.	44.	=
Leadership				
6.	19.	32.	45.	=
Compassion				
7.	20.	33.	46.	=
Wisdom				
8.	21.	34.	47.	=
Knowledge				
9.	22.	35.	48.	=
Faith				
10.	23.	36.	49.	=
Healing				
11.	24.	37.	50.	=
Discernment				
12.	25.	38.	51.	=
Interpretation of Tongues				
13.	26.	39.	52.	=

FOOD FOR THOUGHT

- Were there any surprises on your list of gifts?
- Do you agree or disagree with the results of your assessment? In what way?
- Consider your top three gifts. What is one way you would like to use each of them?
- How would you like God to be using these gifts through you in 10 years?

CHAPTER 7

SPIRITUAL GIFTS DEFINITIONS

"Wisdom is the right use of knowledge. To know is not to be wise. Many men know a great deal, and are all the greater fools for it. There is no fool so great a fool as a knowing fool. But to know how to use knowledge is to have wisdom."

Charles Spurgeon, "The Fourfold Treasure"[8]

Below are definitions and some insight about the individual spiritual gifts. I begin with the literal definition as stated in one or more concordances, and then describe what it may become in practice in your life.

PROPHECY
1 Cor. 14:3; Acts 2:37-40 - the gift of communicating and enforcing revealed truth.

The gift of prophecy enables you to hear the voice of God and speak His words boldly for the strengthening, comfort, and encouragement of others. (The entire next chapter is dedicated to a deeper explanation of this gift.)

SERVING
Acts 6:1-7; Rom 12:7; Gal 6:10 - the gift of 'waiting upon' or doing any form of physical ministry.

People with the gift of serving have unique joy, will-power, and discipline to do any task - whether small or great - in working for the overall good of the body of Christ. Those with the gift of service have a supernatural ability to know and anticipate what is needed, or that which will have the greatest impact for the cause of ministry. If this was one of your top spiritual gifts, you will find great joy by serving those in need as well as the church or places of ministry. God has given you supernatural insight into how to bless others or advance ministry. Be sure to act on these insights by doing what God has placed on your heart to bless individuals. You can also make suggestions to church leadership based on what you see, and what you would be willing to do. A biblical example would be Tabitha, also known as Dorcas, who used her spiritual gift of serving by sewing garments and items for a large group of widows in her town. Her gift was so precious to the widows, that just after she died they showed all she had given them to Peter, who had come to town to preach. He was so moved by the love her gift had aroused in the widows, that he raised Tabitha from the dead.

TEACHING
Eph. 4:12-13; 1 Cor 12:28; Acts 18:24-28 - the ability to share instruction.

The ability to study and learn primarily to bring understanding and depth. The gift of teaching promotes accuracy and excellence. It is primarily related to scriptural revelation and instruction, but it can translate to whatever God wants it to apply. People with this spiritual gift will have a supernatural ability to understand and comprehend accurate truth, and also instruct others within it. A teacher is going to be able to think creatively to not only communicate the concept, but cause the person you are teaching to internalize and understand/apply it. If teaching is one of your top spiritual gifts, you should look for opportunities to instruct others in things that will have significant impact either spiritually or practically. In a church or ministry, you should volunteer wherever teaching is needed; i.e. a small group or a class. A biblical example of someone with the gift of teaching is Luke. As he introduces his gospel, he emphasizes that his desire is for his account to be "perfect" and "orderly." It was very important to him that the receiver - Theophilus - would grow in both his knowledge and certainty.

EXHORTATION
Acts 14:22; Rom 12:8; 1 Tim 4:13 - to call to or encourage.

Exhortation is the ability to encourage others through the written or spoken word and biblical truth. Those with the spiritual gift of exhortation have a supernatural ability to motivate others to take steps of faith or get involved/join in. A person who has been given this gift may say the same thing to someone that others they know have been saying, but this gift from God enables the words to have greater impact.

Also known as the gift of 'encouragement,' this gift can unlock a person's well of courage or impart strength to them to do something they may have been hesitant to do. This gift should not be misconstrued as simply saying nice things about someone as the more banal use of the word "encouragement" can become; nor is it a "rah-rah" speech. It is a prayerful impartation of deep motivation that calls a person or people to take action.

If this was one of your top spiritual gifts, you might find yourself attracted to those who are losing hope or that might be trapped in addiction or patterns of pain or trauma. Don't let yourself be deterred by how many others may have tried to help - but prayerfully seek opportunity to speak into their life. In terms of ministry or church, look to get involved in ministries that restore hope to the hopeless. You will also be immensely useful to any ministry that has inherent value for church leadership but might be struggling to gain involvement. Your presence as a recruiter can have a lasting impact even in areas that may have formerly been struggling. A biblical character with this gift would be Jude. The whole of his book is an exhortation to, *"contend for the faith that was once for all entrusted to God's holy people."* (v. 3) His spiritual gift of exhortation was the platform and mission from which Jude spoke, and inspired others to speak and live their faith.

GIVING
2 Cor. 8:1-7; Mark 12:41-44; Rom 12:8 - to cause or produce/give forth from oneself.

The ability to produce wealth and to give tithes, offerings, or to those in need for the purpose of advancing the Kingdom of God on earth. Those with the spiritual gift of giving are motivated to generously resource others, and will often create income or other assets so more can be given. People with the spiritual gift of giving may also selflessly and joyously give their time to extraordinary proportions utilizing skills they have already acquired to bless or help others and advance the Kingdom of God.

If giving was one of your top spiritual gifts, you should pray that God would stir your imagination to conceive of ways you might give more. When this spiritual gift is given full platform, it can change the lives of many, including yours. Perhaps, there is a business venture of your own that you have not yet conceived? You might find yourself not just giving greater offerings, but potentially creating income opportunities for others. (Note, this is just one possibility. Entrepreneurship is not a requirement for this gift to engage in your life. I'm merely recalling a way I have seen this gift play out in the lives of some.) A biblical character with this gift would likely have been Lydia, who sold fine cloth throughout Rome from the wealthy port city of Macedonia. Upon conversion to Christ, she placed both her home and resources in the hands of Paul to help fund the church and missionary journeys.

LEADERSHIP
Rom 12:8; 1 Tim 3:1-13; Heb 13:17 - the ability to steer or give governance.

The ability to serve and influence people while directing and focusing them on the big picture, vision, or idea. People with the supernatural gift of leadership can listen, inspire, decide, and create effective strategies or systems that further the Kingdom. Those with a supernatural gift of leadership have a great connection to people, and often have a revealed understanding of how people tend to think, act, and what they value. Some with the gift of leadership can build on this revelation to personally motivate and instruct, while others use it to create administrative opportunities for others to engage in a mission or vision; some will do both. The governance aspect of this gift also gives this person a supernatural ability to wisely discern God's will and make hard decisions.

Simply put, if this is one of your top gifts, then you should look to lead others. Your gift will not engage and develop unless you are in a position in which others are following you, particularly in a way that advances the cause of Christ. You do not need to be the ultimate leader, but at least volunteer for a team of individuals who bear the weight of responsibility. In any such environment, your gift will grow and thrive. Biblical characters with the spiritual gift of leadership include many of the most well-known throughout the New Testament; but I will highlight James, who listened to the points of view about circumcision in Acts 15, a debate that seemed to have taken a length of time with little resolution. James takes charge and makes the decision to speak with finality and scriptural authority, which then frees Paul to take his next steps in his missionary journey to the gentiles.

COMPASSION
Matt 9:35-36; Mark 9:41; 1 Thess 5:14 - Mercy, pity, or loyalty to the covenants of God.

The ability to feel empathy and to care for those who are hurting - to understand and empathize deeply. Those with the spiritual gift of compassion visibly fulfill God's promises by choosing to express powerful words and acts of love and kindness, whether or not it seems deserved. The spiritual gift of compassion can create peace in times of conflict, and serve as a deposit from which one can creatively meet needs. The gift of compassion is often undervalued, but it is core to the mission of God and most churches. The Bible records many miraculous acts of Jesus that took place when He was moved with compassion. Many churches have some form of "loving people" as a part of their stated or implied mission or vision. The expression of this love is significantly enhanced by the spiritual gift of compassion.

God can use those with this gift to motivate others to go further in the service of those who are oppressed or poor. They are also genuine peacemakers - able to see and relate to the point of view of many with great empathy. Expressing this empathy can soften the hearts of those involved, and better help them to understand those who may oppose them. If this was one of your top gifts, look for opportunities to serve those in need, especially those that others may overlook or misunderstand. In times of conflict, keep this in mind: Your spiritual gift of compassion is never wrong. So, speak and act according to what God is moving you to say and do, and it can supernaturally shift hearts in hard times. Biblical characters with the spiritual gift of compassion would include John, who stayed at the crucifixion until the very end, and accepted Jesus' request to watch over and care for His mother.

WORD OF WISDOM
1 Cor 12:8 - Words of skillful counsel.

People who have the supernatural gift of words of wisdom will hear God's voice with the specific intent to solve problems or offer advice that cannot be grasped by human strength. Someone with this spiritual gift can be given significant insight into the nature of problems and solutions on subjects or dynamics of which they have no personal knowledge. A word of wisdom can be an encouragement, a warning, or a very practical direction.

If word of wisdom was one of your top gifts, you will find fulfillment in praying for those who are facing difficult circumstances or big decisions. Out of your intercession, allow God to speak to you on their behalf, and boldly speak whatever it is to the person for which you have been praying, even if it does not make sense to you. In a church, look to be a part of prayer ministries, intercessory teams and, perhaps, ministry leadership. Words of wisdom, like words of knowledge that we will speak about in a moment, are not prophecy. They are not restricted to building up, encouraging, and comforting. They certainly can be any of these things, but they can also be strident and to the point. Paul speaks a word of wisdom to the centurion when he told him not to continue sailing on to Phoenix, but should instead remain in Crete. The centurion distrusted Paul's word likely due to the fact Paul was not a sailor. His refusal to heed caused the ship to wreck.

WORD OF KNOWLEDGE
1 Cor 12:8 - Words of practical knowledge.

People who have the supernatural gift of words of knowledge can receive factual insight from God about the unspoken prayer needs of others. Factual knowledge and revelation can also be given about any worldly subject that answers a prayer or serves the purposes of God. Words of knowledge range quite a bit. They can often be about specific needs people have that require prayer or intervention. This is the most commonly utilized it seems. For instance, a minister who receives a "word of knowledge" that someone in a service or meeting is suffering from a particular ailment. The person might then receive prayer for healing. However, a word of knowledge can absolutely be used in almost anything.

Pastor Kris Vallotton, a Senior Associate Pastor at Bethel Church in Redding, CA, shared the following testimony during a training for a church staff on which I served. He shared how God had given him a word of knowledge when he was working as a mechanic about how to fix a truck. It was for his biggest client, and he had researched the issue for days with the master techs of the truck's manufacturer to no avail. With no other options and extremely concerned about his client's potential reaction, he prayed. The Holy Spirit spoke to him and told him there was a broken electrical diode under the truck's right front fender. He opened it up, and there was the broken diode. He repaired it, and the truck started right away.

I've also heard additional testimonies from doctors who were stumped on severe ailments of their patients and, after prayer, would hear diagnoses - which turned out to be correct - that no scan or test had previously revealed. Words of wisdom are counsel, and words of knowledge are facts.

If the spiritual gift of words of knowledge was one of your top gifts, be certain to spend time in prayer as often as you can for those in seemingly impossible need. In your own life, pray about every problem you encounter. The testimony of God's practical, seemingly unknowable facts that lead to various victories are extremely encouraging and speak to God's value of concerning Himself with all that concerns us, as any good Father does. In a church or ministry, consider joining intercessory or prayer teams, and wherever you serve, be a voice that prioritizes prayer any time a seemingly impossible obstacle is encountered.

FAITH
1 Cor 12:9; Acts 3:6; 9:36-43; 28:3 - Belief. Absolute confidence.

People with the supernatural gift of faith are going to have confidence in God's goodness and ability to act, regardless of what is being said or the odds of success. They see the impossible as attainable and will identify what is positive and Godly in the most difficult or desperate circumstances. People with the gift of faith are going to be much more preoccupied with the future and what God will do than what God has not done in the past.

If this was one of your top gifts, then you should be sure to not just pray on your own, but actively seek opportunities to pray with others. When others share with you about a problem or challenge they are facing, get used to asking the question, "Can I pray for you?" Your prayers are supernaturally empowered to encourage and impart faith to those who are in challenging situations. You've probably heard the Chinese proverb, "Better to teach someone to fish than to give them a fish." The gift of faith can reproduce itself by lifting the spirits of those around you, motivating them to take heart and see the caring and powerful hand of God. Perhaps the next time, they may not despair as much. In church or ministry, join prayer teams and lead small groups; join leadership teams, as they face challenging circumstances often and need the positive, supernatural encouragement that your gift of faith can bring. Biblical examples include Barnabas, who encouraged the saints at Antioch and reminded them of God's purpose as 'a good man, full of the Holy Spirit and of faith.'

HEALING
1 Cor 12:9; Acts 5:12-16; Acts 20:7-12 - Complete restoration.

People with the supernatural gift of healing can pray (most common), speak over, or even simply be near people with ailments and cause restoration to take place. The gift of healing can restore tissue, mend a heart, or reverse mental damages and pain. This may be one of the most straightforward of all the spiritual gifts. If this is one of your top spiritual gifts, then pray for those who are sick with the expectation they will be healed. Consider volunteering at a hospital or hospice, or even pursuing a certificate of chaplaincy so you can be admitted to visit hospital patients and pray for them.

There are many books on healing and healing ministry and you should take up reading them. Often, those with the gift of healing are also served well by learning about deliverance ministries, where demons and spirits that oppress others are cast out. Many have experienced healing of chronic diseases when being delivered from such things, so you may also want to ask your pastoral leadership for instruction or mentoring. Consume testimonies of healing and be open to learning more. When you pray for someone, and they are healed, write the testimony down to share with others or to look back on and encourage yourself if ever your prayers for someone's healing are not producing results. In church, join prayer and visitation ministries certainly; however, this is one of those gifts you should be prepared to use whenever and wherever you may be called. It is a "gift of opportunity" in a sense. When the need presents itself, anoint with oil and pray!

DISCERNMENT
1 Cor 12:10; Acts 16:18 - The act of deciding, judging, or passing a sentence on.

People with the spiritual gift of discernment have the supernatural ability to discern the presence and blessing of God, the presence of evil, and that which is not spiritual at all but of human origin. The gift can certainly be useful in spiritual warfare, but its main function brings about wisdom and guidance for those who are pursuing the things of God. A person with a gift of discernment can sense God's delight in someone or an idea they may have, as well as trepidation about something that is not in alignment with what He has purposed. This 'sense' of the Holy Spirit vs. an evil one would often have nothing to do with a person's feelings (and may even be oppositional to them).

In other words, you may find yourself in a discussion about God or ministry or what have you. Perhaps, someone expresses something and, at first, you really like what they are saying or suggesting. But almost immediately after, you get the sense that it is not Godly. The idea may not necessarily be offensive, you just know it is a good human idea but not something God wants everyone to act on. This hypothetical would prove the gift of discernment at work as it is not something that stems from your own personal feelings, but from what the Holy Spirit has revealed to you.

If discernment is one of your top gifts, it is likely a good idea to study about deliverance ministry, as it would be good to obtain biblically sound methods of dealing with evil when you encounter it. Prayer should become an extremely vital and ongoing discipline in your life, as the Spirit may reveal things to you that are not meant to be addressed right in that moment. In church or ministry, your gift may be best utilized if you are either leading or near leadership, where your prayerful insights might help confirm the wisdom and presence of God in times of strategy or planning. In the book of Acts chapter 16, discernment was demonstrated by Paul when his group was being pursued by a possessed female slave. She was shouting that these were men of the 'Most High God,' something that was not only true but some might say was a good thing. Paul allowed this to go on for several days, though he certainly knew this truth was revealed to her demonically. Eventually, exasperated, he casts out the demon.

INTERPRETATION OF TONGUES
1 Cor 12:10 ; 14:5; 14:27 - Ability to interpret "glossa" - the gift of tongues.

A person with this spiritual gift has the supernatural ability to understand the "groanings and utterances" of glossa. It is often a prayerful gift; speaking out what is beautiful and edifying to those who hear it. Someone who has this gift may even produce encouraging words that sound very prophetic - and it's important for someone to properly distinguish if they can interpret a tongue vs. speak a prophetic word. Prophetic words can be spoken at any time that God chooses to speak through someone, but interpretation can obviously only be utilized after tongues are spoken.

If this is one of your top spiritual gifts, you should spend much time praying in tongues on your own in private, and practice interpreting what you are praying. What you hear may sound strange to you, as they are your own expression, yet it is unencumbered by personal or worldly limitations. They may represent your truest calls, your spirit's extolling words about God. Write them down and let them edify and encourage you. In church or ministry, join prayer and intercessory teams and practice this gift with those you trust to help you grow in confidence.

It's important to note that interpretation does not mean translation. In other words, you may feel called to elaborate a bit on the number of words spoken in a tongue so that a group of people in a prayer meeting understand what is being said and can, therefore, be edified. The root word of "interpretation" as used in Corinthians is "hermeneia." It is from this root we also get the word, "hermeneutics" which is the study of correctly interpreting scripture in preparation for teaching or preaching. In the same way preaching is not simply reciting the Bible, but releasing its truth so the hearer can be built up. The interpretation of tongues seeks to build up those present publicly with understanding of what is being communicated in that tongue.

All right, so you have assessed your gifts, and have been given some detail about their nature and usefulness. Now, there's another gift the scriptures encourage all of us to 'seek.' This is the gift of prophecy. We will discover why this gift has so much weight by dedicating the entirety of the next chapter to studying it. Even if prophecy wasn't on your list of gifts from your assessment, it's very important to gain an understanding of how it functions and relates to all of the other spiritual gifts.

Let's continue on.

CHAPTER 8

STARTERFLUID

"God's word in your mouth is just as powerful as God's word in His own mouth."

Pastor Melodie Leake, Allison Park Church

I'm sure Lydia up there in Macedonia had these thoughts and feelings...maybe they came to her as she picked up the random cups and other pottery utensils from about her living room as she headed into the kitchen to wash them up. She may have been reflecting on the evening after her brothers and sisters in The Way had left her house to return to their own dwellings after church. Perhaps now and then she just thought, "Something seemed to have been missing tonight..."

I'd wager there was, at least, one occasion where Justas Jonas expressed ardent support and affirmation of another masterful sermon by his dear friend, Martin Luther, as they headed to the pub some Sunday evening. But, quietly, he nevertheless thought, "Overall, church sure wasn't as exciting as it used to be when we first started this thing."

I'd bet Puritan John Winthrop left church one day on his way back to his Massachusetts Bay home and couldn't help thinking, "People seem bored by these sermons about prayer. Perhaps I need to start a new series...or maybe we need to add something to the worship team besides the lute. I don't know...it just felt kind of dead in there today."

In every Christian gathering that has ever happened in the history of the Church on our planet, the leader of that meeting and most of the participants have hoped God would be present, and that the experience would have a significant impact on hearts and minds. I can't necessarily quantify it, but I'm pretty sure many such leaders and attendees have left with, at least, some level of disappointment. This has likely been the case, regardless of the denominational or spiritual structure involved.

We all want the fire of the Holy Spirit in our worship services and prayer gatherings; but I think, often, the very best tool God has given us to start that fire goes largely unused during these times.

I'm speaking of the spiritual gift of prophecy.

Sure-

It's been misused.
It's been very misunderstood.

Mostly, I would say it has been simply ignored. It's like we have a bag of BBQ charcoal we just bought and the package (like they always do) says, "Just one match lights it up! No starter fluid needed!" Which, of course, anyone who has spent any time in pursuit of the title of local neighborhood "grill master" knows is a bitter, bold-faced lie. Instead of all the gyrations and struggles and frustrations many go through to try to live up to the declaration on the package, sometimes it's just better to break down and use a little starter fluid to get cookin'.

In 1 Corinthians, Paul gives all of us the spiritual "starter fluid" for the flow of gifting and dynamic interaction with God, and it centers on the gift of prophecy. Obviously, if this was one of your top spiritual gifts, then it is vital for you to begin to put some of the principles I will be outlining into practice as soon as you are able. However, the reason I've given this gift its own chapter is because it is really important that all of us grow in our understanding of this gift and how we should pursue it.

First off, let's give a little more detailed definition of prophecy, as provided to us by Jesus:

> "I have much more to say to you, more than you can now bear. But when he, the Spirit of truth, comes, he will guide you into all the truth. He will not speak on his own; he will speak only what he hears, and he

will tell you what is yet to come. He will glorify me because it is from me that he will receive what he will make known to you. All that belongs to the Father is mine. That is why I said the Spirit will receive from me what he will make known to you." John 16:12-15

Right here, Jesus explains to the disciples several aspects of this gift. First, He emphasizes again how He and the Spirit are one, and how the words the Spirit speaks to us are the words of Jesus Himself as given to Him by the Father. Quite simply, prophecy, therefore, are the words of God (all three persons) given to us. So, if you have the gift of prophecy, you have been given a supernatural ability to hear God's words and share them with others.

Let's break down a few features of what prophetic words are like, and how they are expressed:

- Prophetic words are not scripture, but they are God's words.

  "For the word of God is alive and active. Sharper than any double-edged sword, it penetrates even to dividing soul and spirit, joints and marrow; it judges the thoughts and attitudes of the heart." Hebrews 4:12

  Scripture stands alone as being useful in teaching, training, and rebuking. However, prophetic words are life-giving and activate faith. So it needs to be spoken!

  One of my pastors, Melodie Leake, says it like this: "God's word in your mouth is as powerful as God's word in His own mouth."

However, it must never disagree with the precepts of scripture or what it teaches:

"But even if we, or an angel from heaven, should preach to you a gospel contrary to what we have preached to you, he is to be accursed." Galatians 1:8

- Prophetic words can be predictive.

Look again at that verse from John 16. In it, Jesus says, *"he will tell you what is yet to come."* (v.13) Often, prophetic words and visions let someone know about God's plans or visions for someone's life. These can be big things or small things, and can range from the immediate future to many, many years later. Often, prophecy can be predictive and long-range.

After I came to Christ, I joined a small group that met on my college campus and was composed mainly of students from the university I attended. The leader of this group had a strong prophetic gift, and the Holy Spirit flowed freely among us. We all spoke prophetic words and encouragement over one another in prayer. Sometimes, our 90-minute time frame stretched for several hours because we were so filled and joyous - singing and praying, and enjoying speaking life over one another.

In this group, I remember there was a young man named John who was currently working as a photographer. He received a prophetic word something like, "Right now you are designing pictures but one day soon you will be creating buildings. Fear not, for this will bring you great joy and your needs will be met." A few years later, due to an economic downturn and some challenges in his business, he closed his studio with no immediate plan. However, through a church connection, he found work as a contractor. The work paid him very well, and though it wasn't something he had considered doing in the past, he found he really enjoyed it, even more than the photography business.

On a few occasions, another young man named Lorne came to the group. Like many of us, he was a theater major. Lorne was very gifted musically, and came from an impoverished background. Someone spoke to him a really unique word that grew from a prophetic vision which stated that God was going to bring financial blessing through his career that would transform the experience of his family for generations to come. But the vision showed him dressed in a suit and in an office, and speaking French. I remember Lorne didn't know what to make of that at the time (and didn't really like the suit part). However, just a few years ago, a mutual friend, who is an actor, ran into him. My friend informed me that he came upon Lorne at an audition he took in New York. Lorne was the director of the show, and he was currently living in Paris. His job was to arrange the music for large scale musicals performed on a popular cruise line. He expressed how thankful he was that God had blessed him and his family more than he could ever have dreamed, but lamented that working for the cruise line could sometimes feel a little "corporate" and that he didn't like having to wear a "suit at the office."

My stories of predictive words, from the lives of others as well as my own, could literally go on and on - every one of them more amazing than the last. When you recall the words that were spoken over you years before at the moment of their fulfillment, it can reinforce faith in a way that few other experiences can outside of witnessing a spontaneous miracle.

- Prophetic words in the New Testament are always strengthening, encouraging, and comforting.

"But the one who prophesies speaks to people for their strengthening, encouragement, and comfort." - 1 Corinthians 14:3

In the Old Testament, prophets were utilized by God to profess His will, including His judgments to the nations of the world and to the Jewish people of God. It was the only source of direct revelation from God. Jesus had not performed His ministry yet. There was no mediator, no helper...just the raw life of an ethnic people to whom God chose to bless with His favor. Therefore, the strident words of the Old Testament prophet were necessary to guide and give the parameters of God's message to His people with no incarnate Word to have revealed it to us.

Two facts changed this dynamic:
1. The fullness of the grace of Jesus was released into the world after His death and resurrection.
2. The church was born at Pentecost, replacing an ethnic vessel (Jews) with anyone (Jews and others) who has received the grace of Jesus to become adopted sons and daughters of God.

The New Testament now teaches us that the gift of prophecy has shifted a bit as Christ speaks to His bride to carry out His mission and His message, as opposed to a world that largely ignored Him. Therefore, the prophetic words that are spoken today are going to be encouraging, comforting, and will build someone up.

When these edifying words are spoken with specificity into the lives of those who are seeking Him it is, at least, deeply stirring. When they are the kinds of things that only God could know, they are immensely faith-building. And, in a world that so often tears down and destroys rather than encourages, a literal "sanctuary" full of people that speak deeply spiritual, meaningful encouragement continuously turns every meeting place into a hot temple of the Holy Spirit, and every casual gathering into an unforgettable connection with the eternal.

As this is the case, anyone can (and should) pursue prophecy!

"Follow the way of love and eagerly desire gifts of the Spirit, especially prophecy." 1 Cor 14:1
"For you can all prophesy in turn so that everyone may be instructed and encouraged." 1 Cor 14:31

So, all of us should keep the love of God in front of us - knowing that prophecy is a key way that His love is expressed. And all of us should seek to express this love.

We can all begin to practice this. You can start simply by praying for someone and while doing so, waiting and listening for a thought, word, or picture that can express something positive and encouraging about that person. Anyone can be encouraging! That's not hard, right? And that's how it starts. It can be a very simple word or phrase, or a simple description of a vision you see in your mind's eye. It can be, in many ways, the easiest of the spiritual gifts to enter into and execute. Because it is so deeply encouraging, it can also act as a sort of fire starter for the other gifts to begin to flow more freely.

Prophecy is my strongest spiritual gift. I am most fulfilled when I spend hours prophesying over others, revealing gifts, affirming and building up faith, and imparting courage to believe in the destinies God has placed before others. It's an absolute love-pouring-out-fest when God gets me started. But I have had decades of practice and study of the subject and of God's word. You may already be right here with me. That's so great! Regardless of whether this is a regular part of your experience, I believe you can and will be there one day if it is an earnest desire for which you are willing to seek and pour out your heart.

You may be thinking, "how do you start the starter fluid?"

Well, activation of prophetic gifts is an extensive process worthy of many books (and many have been written).

But, if prophecy is one of your top gifts, let's start with some basics:

First, here are the three parts of a prophetic word:

1. Revelation: The first thing that happens is while you are praying for someone, God speaks to you about something you have no earthly knowledge about. This can be delivered to you in many forms: a vision, mental pictures, words written in front of you that you can read, or an audible voice to name some of the most common.
2. Interpretation: When giving a verbal word, the person who is receiving the word is ultimately responsible for the interpretation. However, when it comes to visions, it's important for you to be able to describe accurately what you are seeing. Sometimes in this instance, the Holy Spirit will declare in your spirit, "And this is what this means..." In that instance, you may be providing "interpretation" but it is only as much as what the Holy Spirit

tells you about the picture or vision He has asked you to share and describe.

3. Application: The final part is, again, ultimately up to the hearer. They need to use what they interpret to help them know what actions to take and how it applies to their life. However, just as with interpretation, God may say, "And this is what I want you to do (how I want you to apply this)." In this instance, you need to speak faithfully what you hear God saying.

Here are my recommendations for how to hear and execute those three parts more often and more accurately as time goes on:

- Pray and read the Bible every day when you first get up. (Yeah, I know, most pastors are nice enough to say, "Well, if you're not a morning person…" I'm sorry - but I'm not that nice of a pastor!) If you're reading this, prophecy is a gift that you want to have added to you, right? If you have it, you want to have more added to you, right? Well, "seek Him first" and it will be added. Seek other things first and they will. Do you want this or not? Get up before everyone else in your house does and place Him before any of your other thoughts or business. Period.

- Worship daily and make fasting a lifestyle. If you want to clearly hear the words of God with accuracy, you need to hone it by spending time in His presence and using the tools God has given you to help overcome those things that stand between you and Him. Fasting can help clear out the "gunk" of this world that can stop the flow of His words through you.

- Practice quieting yourself in prayer and listening to Him. Write down what you hear. It may be for you, or it may be for someone else. If it is for someone else - and it builds up, strengthens, or encourages - share it with that person.

If it is more of a warning or concern, then you are being called to intercede and pray for them.

- Practice, practice, practice. Get around Spirit-filled believers and share what God tells you.

But what if I hear wrong?

This is, by far, the biggest question I hear when I teach on prophecy. Let's look at the answer:

> "Do not quench the Spirit. Do not treat prophecies with contempt but test them all; hold on to what is good, reject every kind of evil." - 1 Thess 5:19-21

First, we need to not let our own self-doubt or insecurity keep us from speaking that which we believe God is saying. This is really the only sure way to "quench" the fire that our "prophetic starter fluid" began. No words = No fire.

Second, it's the responsibility of the person who has received the word to pray over the word and discern its truth.

Third, it's likely you may get it wrong now and then. However, if you are disciplined to make sure it builds up, encourages, and comforts; and that it does not conflict with the precepts of scripture, it's likely not going to be as damaging as if you had "quenched the spirit" and never spoke it to begin with.

Several years ago, I received a word from a well-known prophet with my two daughters in front of a church. It was a great and encouraging word. At the time my girls, Isabella and Galilee, were about 13 and 8 years of age, respectively. Over Isabella, he spoke that she would be called into the scientific field and help those who were sick. Over Galilee, he said she would go into the arts and education.

Today, Isabella, who just graduated from ministry

school, is now 22 and will be taking some further college in video game development - the discipline of those who create the world and the story and the art - almost like a production designer does for movies. She also has a dream of one day starting a school, perhaps in the mission field.

Galilee is heading into her senior year of high school and is beginning her college tours to pursue an undergraduate degree in biology with the intent of one day being a Physician's Assistant.

So, the prophet did get the predictive word wrong in terms of which child would do what. He got his spiritual wires crossed for a moment. However, he was right in that he heard from the Holy Spirit - and quite accurately - as to what my children were called to do.

We prayed over and stood on the words this prophet spoke, and as time unfolded, we began to see which word was intended for which child. No harm done.

Speaking of standing on a word and discerning it, here's a great exercise to engage in when you receive a prophetic word:

1. Make sure you try to record it as it is being said. Grab your phone and hit record on voice memo or the camera.
2. Type it out. Transcribe it word for word.
3. Read it through and pray over it.
4. Take three different highlighter pens. As you continue to pray over it, use a different color highlighter to highlight each of the following:
   a. The things that God says He's going to do. These are things where there is nothing you can do. It's something that only God can make happen and doesn't require anything of you. For instance: "God says He is going to give you a financial blessing from a com-

pletely unknown source." This is something you can't make happen. It's just something God will do.

b. The things that indicate something you must do. "God says He is going to raise you up into higher education - I see many degrees on your wall." If God were to speak this over you, you should probably make plans to go to college. You would need to study in school and apply to a university.

c. Things that seem like it may be a little of both. "God says he is going to move in someone's heart to give you a new opportunity soon that will advance His will in your life. So be on-watch! Be intentional and invest time, energy, and hospitality into people that you meet for the first time over the next several months." If this were spoken over you, it's something that God says He is going to do, but He is also telling you to do something as well.

I have a collection of many prophetic words in a large file with which I have done this exercise. Periodically, I take them out and look them over. I pray over them again and look to see what has been fulfilled, and remind myself of the things God has declared over me. This is always really enjoyable! It's being encouraged all over again! Doing so also reminds me of the things I need to continue to pray about and declare.

Occasionally, I have some words that are so way off base - so completely different from anything that God has ever done in my life, or that which God has ever given me any desire to pursue - that I simply let them go. I don't hold anything against whoever spoke it over me. Rather, I'm thankful that they loved God enough to express His love toward me through prophecy. In keeping this perspective, I am doing my best to fulfill the counsel of Jesus as expressed in Matthew

10:41: *"Whoever welcomes a prophet as a prophet will receive a prophet's reward."*

Bottom line: I'm just thankful for anyone that cares about God and has the passion and love in their heart to pour out some starter fluid into the life of someone else - especially you!

FOOD FOR THOUGHT
- How do you most often hear from God? Is it: An audible voice? A vision? A dream? Do you see words in front of you like God wrote it? Does God bring scripture to mind?
- Have you ever received a prophetic word? If so, which is currently the most meaningful that you recall? Why is it so?
- Have you ever had a "predictive" word spoken over you? Has it been fulfilled yet or not? In what way or ways?

CHAPTER 9

TRANSFORMATION SEQUENCE

"It's a five star matchup because we're in it!"

James Farrior
Pittsburgh Steelers Inside Linebacker
Just before Super Bowl XLIII

Now that you have discovered your spiritual gifts on paper, it's time to get the right mindset for what comes next and discuss practical steps for getting started using them. God isn't in the habit of creating paper heroes. He formed you and revealed your gifts so you might function with real, supernatural power to change the spiritual and even physical realities of our world.

Speaking of heroes, most, if not all, first-run and pre-quel superhero movies (as well as most first-person adventure video games) contain what is known in the screenwriting biz as "The Transformation Sequence." This is the part of the movie where our (typically scrawny or nerdy or otherwise misfit) protagonist discovers he or she can do things other people can't. This usually happens in a moment of passion or stress when the young hero is being bullied or someone they love is in danger, and this sudden strange phenomenal ability saves the day (and usually freaks out our hero). I'm sure you've seen it a thousand times…Whether it's Peter Parker's incredible arachnid-inspired agility caused by a spider bite, or simple freak genetics of mutants like Wolverine that cause super strength and claws to grow out of knuckles, or even the fairly unexplained digital talent of Neo in *The Matrix*, most of us have seen this play out repeatedly in the last several decades.

In fact, some of these movies have been remade with nearly the same story lines and characters but with different actors - and only a few years apart! It's a near obsession in our culture, honestly. It's almost hard to believe, but, according to IMDB, as of the writing of this book and since the afore-mentioned character of Neo first appeared in *The Matrix* in 1999, there have been a total of *165 feature films* released into theaters that follow a superhero theme, and it's likely that the vast majority of these have some aspect of a transformation sequence in their plots. That's a whole lot of supernatural gift discovery!

Of course, there's likely a shelf-life to this pattern in our popular media. (But, it's actually hard to say when that might be!) Personally, I think the long-standing run of these sorts of stories speaks to an innate and unrealized desire within humans. We want to participate in something extraordinary. We each have a subconscious remnant of our eternal connection to God, which manifests in the belief that there must be something beyond living and dying in a reality that is completely confined by human limitation. I would argue that for those of us whose consciousness of God has awakened to where we worship, love, and serve Him as our all-powerful and supernatural Father, we should actually *lead the way* in this belief.

Now, we've already spoken extensively on God's true heart of love and His creation that fuels the faith needed for participation in spiritual gifts. This love and honor of others should produce a significant amount of humility. But don't let anyone tell you that desiring to have a great impact and be used by God through your spiritual gifts in a great way is somehow sinful. Don't let someone convince you that the longing you have to be a "hero" of our faith is purely a selfish ambition that you must eradicate. This is not only an inappropriate accusation - it's an un-biblical one as well.

Yes, I know...you've heard it said and maybe you've even been tempted to think something like, "All of this talk of superheroes and supernatural ability that we participate in by our own will is just childish."

To which I say, "Oh really? 'Childish?'...

Huh…

…What an interesting choice of words."

Let's look at Matthew 18:1-4:

(First- it's important to note that in the days leading up to this moment, the disciples had been sent out by Jesus where they drove out many demons, healed many people, and even pulled money out of a fish's mouth to pay their taxes.)

> "At that time the disciples came to Jesus and asked, 'Who, then, is the greatest in the kingdom of heaven?' He called a little child to him, and placed the child among them. And he said: 'Truly I tell you, unless you change and become like little children, you will never enter the kingdom of heaven. Therefore, whoever takes the lowly position of this child is the greatest in the kingdom of heaven.'"

You know what I think is the most conspicuous part of what Jesus says here?

He never rebukes the disciples for wanting to be great.

He certainly could have. It sounds arrogant when you read what they said. I mean, the question of which one of them would be the "greatest" certainly sounds like something Mohammed Ali in his pugilistic prime would ask if he could. Instead, Jesus shows them a better way. In fact, He answers them very directly by giving them the key to greatness. And what was that key?...

...to become like a child...

...to be more "child-like" and less "adult-like".

Sure, this obviously speaks to humility. Jesus even uses phrasing to emphasize taking a "low position." He also refers to means by which we are able to enter into the kingdom - and we know that is only accomplished by faith.

Therefore, how do we become "greatest in the kingdom of heaven?" We need the faith of a childlike person - and

NOT the "sensible" questioning/resistance of an adult-like person.

Put another way:

Childlike people believe God because He said it and they, therefore, experience a supernatural life. Whereas, adult-like people believe God only after they experience it and, therefore,

...they never live supernaturally at all.

Life (and greatness) in the Kingdom of heaven isn't about what you know or what you say you know, it's all about experience.

The last chapters where you discovered your gifts and learned a bit about what they are was a bit like Christmas morning and the tree was full of gifts. Now, it's the day after. School's not in session, there's plenty of leftovers, it dumped snow last night, and your only task today is to play and play and play.

In other words, now that you've identified your spiritual gifts and prayed to grasp a better understanding of their meaning, you're likely realizing you've started your very own transformation sequence. Even more, hopefully, you're gaining the faith to ask God:

"So, which of us can be the greatest superhero in the kingdom of heaven?"

The ability to heal diseases, send demons back to hell, see into people's beautiful future and encourage the deepest parts of people's spirits is a whole lot better (and more useful) than some gnarly claws or sticky string flying out of your wrists, am I right?

But we're not quite done identifying/exploring how God made you just yet. Because, you see - it's not just that God has given you gifts...

You are a gift.

Soon it will be time to open yourself up and find out what kind of gift you've been created to be - at a deep, deep place in your spirit.

FOOD FOR THOUGHT

- What was the best gift you ever received as a child and what made it so? How about when you were an adult?
- If you are reading this with others, what gift would you give each other if you could? If you're reading on your own, who is one person would you give a gift to right now, and what would it be?
- Consider your top spiritual gifts. Is there anything that holds you back from using them? How do you think the opinions of others are influencing you in this?

CHAPTER 10

ASSEMBLE THE AVENGERS

"You would not have called to me had I not been calling to
you."

"The Silver Chair" by C.S. Lewis[9]

The Hunger Games.
The Divergent Series.
Percy Jackson.
The Maze Runner.
The Harry Potter Series.

What do all of these incredibly popular movie and book series have in common, besides billions and billions of dollars generated by the billions of readers and viewers?

Each one of these epic stories contains an element where each person either chooses or is placed into a tribe, faction, house, etc. In each of the cases, most of the characters embrace this placement as a portion of their identity, family, or community. Even in the *Divergent* series where the main character, Beatrice Prior, is targeted because she is a super-hero like combination of all of the traits of the various factions, she goes through sequences of confusion and angst over her true purpose, and bouts of loneliness when she is desiring to find her place in life.

On the one hand, the overwhelming success of these series is intriguing to me. I think most people spend time resisting "labels" others might place on them. We each want to be seen as individuals, and we certainly don't want to be forced into a category. On the other hand, I also observe there is a desire we share to embrace a specific group that shares common values and abilities. Clubs, societies, teams, meet-up groups, unions, etc. are all examples of this and they are nearly as old as time.

If you've seen any of the movies above, I would bet you've wondered which District you might have fared best in, or whether you would have been placed in 'Erudite' or 'Dauntless.' You can go online or to your local mall right now and purchase all sorts of garments, banners, and even office supplies that let the real world know that your fictitious self would be a proud member of 'Griffendor.'

God knows about this desire His children have to identify with a community or people that transcends appearance and geography. He knows that we each want our identities to deepen beyond a label to a shared purpose. He understood that we each ideally desire an identity that is unique, but also does not stand alone in a vacuum without purpose or effect. We simultaneously find strength and comfort in being with those we share a great deal in common with, while also powerfully attracted to those who are different from us. Most of us are curiously intrigued by how we all best work together.

To this end, there is one more test for you to take. This one isn't as challenging or involved or as lengthy as the last one, but it does point to something within you that is deeper than the spiritual gifts. It's your core identity or "calling." Every one of us has one. It doesn't matter if you have ever been to Bible college or not. It doesn't matter how long you have had faith in Christ. It doesn't matter if you've ever served in a church or even if you've ever attended one. Every son and daughter of God has a calling, or ultimate purpose, in Christ.

In the book of Ephesians, Paul names these callings as Apostle, Prophet, Pastor, Teacher, and Evangelist. He does so in chapter 4, verse 11. Many believers interpret these verses (with some sound reasoning) to be those who set aside all other pursuits and serve the church directly. However, my life and study leads me in a slightly different direction. I understand where those that feel that way are coming from, but I believe it is too narrow a point of view that doesn't match the entire context of what is being taught in Ephesians 4. Let's break this down:

First - let's go ahead and quote the famous verse that names these ministries, functions, callings, or "folds" (that term I never have understood, but I digress) whatever you want to call them...here it is from Eph 4:11-12:

"So Christ himself gave the apostles, the prophets, the evangelists, the pastors and teachers, to equip his people for works of service, so that the body of Christ may be built up."

The logic of those who think these only refer to some sort of 'higher' class of 'called folks' goes that the phrase, "equip his people for works of service" denotes a separation from those who 'aren't' one of these things.

However, in my view, several verses before this, he begins to lay an inclusive foundation as to whom he is exactly referring when he states in Ephesians 4:7, *"**But to each one** of us grace has been given as Christ apportioned it."*

Unfortunately, I think many westerners have erroneously reserved "us" in that sentence to mean those in some sort of professional clergy; meaning only those who are employed by (or at least pronounced with some sort of title) by the church as those who might fulfill these callings. But he actually does not specify any group, in particular (let alone some sort of until-that-time non-existent spiritual 'rank.') It's also illogical to think Paul would have had any reason or thought to do so - the church of Jesus in his day wasn't exactly a highly structured, well-funded organization.

Then, Paul shifts his context even more when he builds on that verse by quoting Psalm 68:

"When he ascended on high,
He led the captives in his train,
And gave gifts to men."

And then he continues:

> "What does 'he ascended' mean except that he also descended to the lower, earthly regions? He who descended is the very one who ascended higher than all the heavens, in order to fill the whole universe. So Christ himself gave the apostles, the prophets, the evangelists, the pastors and teachers, to equip his people for works of service…" (v. 9-12)

He explains the ministry of Jesus as the one who conquered death in its full form here on earth, and His ascension above all, and His current omnipresence. Paul is using this to get to his real meaning, which is not trying to develop an enduring church hierarchy. Rather, he's on a completely different subject. He's emphasizing Christ's unified nature with the Holy Spirit so that he can declare that Jesus, Himself, is the one who appointed the following callings (apostle, prophet, evangelists, pastors, and teachers) upon the "us" that he referred to when he began the thought back in verse 7. He was obviously most interested in making sure the Ephesians didn't go the way that so many in the early church tried to splinter into (and still exists in some circles today) with various denials about Christ's deity or a polytheistic (multi-god) faith. There was danger of this happening as people became aware of the power of God through the Holy Spirit.

A few verses later, Paul further confirms this point of view when he changes his "us" into a "we" as he explains the outcome of what Jesus has done by appointing people in this way:

> "Then we will no longer be infants, tossed back and forth by the waves." (v. 14)

There's no reason to think Paul was referring to himself and the other apostles or church leaders when he said "us," but then shifts to "we" (meaning everyone) when He talks about how we will all be mature and no longer infantile.

In light of this, I find it an error to interpret the language here as some sort of specification of certain conditions for individuals to be apostles, or prophets, or evangelists, or pastors, or teachers and some category of 'everyone else' left out. These are the 'callings' with which we all participate in an effort to build up the body of Christ. In wealthier nations and cultures, some people are so blessed as to live out these callings as their sole means of support. Also, there may be some whose commitment to these callings becomes such a passion, and the fruit of their labor grows so significantly, that it dominates anything else they may set time and effort to. Hence, your local congregation may have a 'pastor,' a mission agency may be led by an 'evangelist,' etc. and I do believe there is an 'office' to be held by people. This office is more of a practical function. A church, denomination, or group of God-fearing men and women confirm that this person is so 'called' in a particular function that they should spend as much of their time as possible doing the work of 'equipping the saints.' This is a significant pronouncement that typically will require a good deal of personal sacrifice, and would be confirmed by spiritual fruit and very high character.

However, I just can't see the existence of this logical, almost natural progression of the purpose of certain people's lives fully eclipsing the idea that all of us - every one of us - YOU - have a core 'calling' of your own whether you are in a church-based ministry role or not.

I didn't invent, nor am I alone in this understanding. John Wimber - the founder of what became known as "The Vineyard Movement," a world sweeping revival of church planting and release of the power of the Holy Spirit that began in the late 1970's - often summed up this same belief by declaring, "Everybody gets to play!" His biography (incidentally, using that phrase as its title) explains that he was leading services in the thousands throughout the world and signs and wonders were poured out wherever he was. Unlike many other revivalists until that time, however, he believed that God could use anyone to do what he was doing. So, instead of setting up bigger and bigger tents or renting bigger and bigger venues, he chose instead to train others and impart, reveal, and commission others to do the ministry he had been a part of. As a result, there are over 2400 Vineyard churches today in 95 countries, and they are continuing to grow.

Anyway - let's get back to the real reason God told me to write this book…

YOU.

Let's look at verse 11 again:

> "So Christ himself gave the apostles, the prophets, the evangelists, the pastors and teachers, to equip his people for works of service…"

Remember how I said in the last chapter that you don't just have gifts, but that you are a gift? This is what I was referring to. As an overarching calling - a portion of your identity - you are an apostle, a prophet, an evangelist, a pastor, or a teacher given to others. You may not have ever seen yourself in this way, but it really is the truth.

I feel part of my job now is to help you gain some confidence in believing in yourself in this way. We're going to go pretty deep here, so let me begin by reminding you of our value of remaining disciplined and true to the biblical lists of gifts. We do this to be sure the gifts we are talking about are, in fact, spiritual and not merely of human skill.

With that in mind, let's elaborate a bit more: It's often the case that many spiritual gift exams and perspectives conflate the verses in Ephesians 4 with the passages we studied in Romans and Corinthians (the lists of spiritual gifts). While I'm glad for any church or leader that embraces and teaches spiritual gifting as a core tool in the arsenal of God's strategy to reach the world, I do think this lack of distinction has brought about some unintended consequences.

Specifically, I think if you simply add, "apostle, prophet, pastor, teacher, and evangelist" (or evangelism) to the list of spiritual gifts you're asking people to identify, you're not only missing the context of Ephesians 4, you are actually sowing confusion and even some significant lethargy to the church.

While I think this applies to any of the five callings, I think the most evident example of this is in our adding the 'spiritual gift' of 'evangelism' to our lists. I hate to break it to you...but it's just not there. I don't personally believe anyone alive has the spiritual gift of evangelism. Why? Because it does not exist, and the suggestion that it does undermines the great commission.

Don't get me wrong, there are "gifted" evangelists - but they are not gifted with evangelism. They're calling and passion for evangelism is a gift to the whole body of Christ. They may use their actual spiritual gifts of mercy, or administration, or teaching, or prophecy (or whatever they've been gifted with) most often, and perhaps even exclusively, among those who are not yet saved. But that is an outgrowth of who they are and not a particular supernatural gift.

As I see it, this conflation has two main consequences:

First, the Christian who is not an evangelist nor identified as having this (non-existent) gift (when in the company of others who have), may have a tendency to leave the sharing of their faith to those who have been identified as such. But Matthew 28 is abundantly clear that the mandate is for all of us to, *"go and make disciples of all nations, baptizing them in the name of the Father and of the Son and of the Holy Spirit"*. 1 Peter 3:15 gets even more personal, instructing all of us no matter what or who we are to, *"be prepared to tell everyone why you believe as you do.."(NLT)*. In a healthy body of Christ, we will allow those who have been identified with certain spiritual gifts to function within them, and encourage them to serve according to these gifts. But, if we lump 'evangelism' into this, we can't be surprised when people who are not identified with this 'gifting' hesitate to share their faith. Like on many other occasions, they may have a tendency to leave that to those who have.

Second, the actual person with the calling of evangelist (that has also likely been taught they have an 'evangelism' gift) may falsely assume that their ability to share the gospel, itself, is somehow more inherently powerful than someone who has not been blessed with this gift. This may cause a lack of growth and refinement in their actual gifting of teaching or skills of communication. It could also cause them to abandon other actual spiritual gifts they have been given that would help them succeed in their calling and purpose to see people come to Christ.

Inherently, most church leaders know the passages in Romans, Corinthians, and Ephesians are not really speaking from the same premise. You know how I know? When was the last time you saw a standard spiritual gift exam with the gift of "Apostle-ism" on it? We kind of get that being an apostle (or apostolic), being a person that develops and sends people into their callings, involves much more than one specific gift (and just a bit of authority as well). This is, I believe, the correct perspective. I would argue, therefore, this perspective should apply to the other callings as well. Someone can (and should) prophesy without necessarily being a prophet, teach without being a teacher, care for and disciple others without being a pastor, share their faith without being an evangelist, and encourage and celebrate others in their destiny without being an apostle. This is because these are things the Bible admonishes us all to do regardless of our gifting. The composite of all of our actual spiritual gifts will help us fulfill our true purpose in the end.

In light of this, you may be asking:

"Why, then, if I should be prepared to do all of these things, whether I am gifted with them or not, is it important to know which of these 5 gifts (callings) you are?"

Well, there are several reasons. First, just as the verses we just studied imply - this knowledge is key to best fulfilling your role in God's plan to build up the body of Christ and to equip your fellow brothers and sisters to do what God has called them to do. (Like we said, this isn't just your pastor's job. It's all of ours.) As a full time pastor in ministry, I can tell you one of the most disappointing tendencies I face in the people I serve is how they call to inform me of problems among our people "just so I'm aware" with no intent in their heart to lift a finger of their own to do anything about it. I usually take this opportunity to 'intensely disciple' and re-frame their mission in the body by pointing out to them how they may better serve alongside me. There are times when this effort is not received. Why? There may be many reasons, but surely one of them is because this person has never identified the calling they have or the gift God has intended them to be for the church.

Second, knowing your calling will help you maintain joy in serving God in what you do wherever you are. Two people may score the same combination of spiritual gifts on their examinations but only find fulfillment in using them by serving in very different ways. Some may feel a deep fulfillment in using their gifts when discipling youth in their local church congregation (like a pastor) and another may not find any motivation to do something like that at all, but will work extra hours at their job every year to pay for a mission trip and do the same thing with adults who never heard about Christ (like an evangelist). This will become more clear to you as we define what these callings mean, and what they look like both as a matter of a role in ministry as well as what it looks like as a matter of personhood.

Third, knowing your 'calling' can even help you focus, in certain circumstances, on the most effective way to serve Christ in your career in the marketplace and even within your own family. This, again, will become more clear as we define what each of these callings as stated by Paul mean and how they function.

So, let's get on with the test, and then we'll come back and define/explain the various callings and how they function together.

THE CALLING/IDENTITY TEST

This test is shorter and a bit more straightforward than the gifts test, and you'll likely latch on to the direction of the questions with more ease. This is perfectly fine. What is most important is for you to pray for a few moments; be sure any distractions around you have been eliminated and that your spirit is quiet before taking this exam. Try to picture and imagine the scenarios as accurately as you can. Then, most importantly, answer as honestly as you are able. Don't try to choose the 'right' answer or the one you think you 'should' choose. Decide based on what you truly, most deeply believe about yourself.

Place a check-mark next to the ONE most likely response to each question/scenario:

1. If I were to be moved to tears, it most likely be for the following reason:
   a. I shared why I believe in Jesus with someone, and they committed their lives to Christ.
   b. A couple I hadn't seen in years told me that something I shared with them about what the Lord had taught me ended up saving their marriage.
   c. A friend told me that if it weren't for all of the prayers I prayed and the things I had done for them, they weren't sure they would have survived the death of their family member.
   d. A church leader who had led hundreds of people to faith came up to me and said that if it were not for a prophetic word I spoke over them years ago, they would never have had the courage to speak about Jesus.
   e. A new Christian I took 'under my wing' years ago and recommended to several people, schools, jobs, etc... went on to create a very large ministry of their own. At a very well attended event, they publicly thanked me, specifically, as the one responsible for getting them launched into their dream.

2. My favorite event at my church is (or would be):
    a. "Bring a friend" services or events and the outreaches we do in our community.
    b. Bible study or any group where we really learn something or share what we are learning.
    c. Life groups with my friends and any time we care for those who are hurting or in need.
    d. Extended worship services where we are encouraged to speak life into one another and share what we believe God is saying.
    e. Whenever we hear from our missionaries, church planters, and are given a chance to sow into their ministries/pray over and commission them.

3. If I ran my own successful company, the best measure of my success at my retirement would be:
    a. I kept adding brand new customers every single year no matter what, and now there are just too many to name. As a result, our company grew from something really small into something extremely prosperous for all of us.
    b. I am recognized as one of the best in our industry at training other people to do what we do, and my own people pour out cards and letters thanking me for everything they learned from me over the years and the difference it has made.
    c. My employees ranked our company as one of the best communities to work for in our city year after year. We've been through it and held together, and they tell me we really are like a family to them.
    d. My company is recognized across the board as an admired trendsetter, and business blogs stated the secret of our success was our ability to be ten steps ahead while always hiring the right person for the

right job every time.

e. Many of those I gave their first break to and developed over the years have gone on to do great things of their own, and they come to my retirement to thank me, Personally.

4. When I think about raising my kids (or the kids I already raised, or kids I imagine raising) one of the most important things to me is/was/would be:

a. That our home is the place where their friends would gather, so we could maintain a Godly atmosphere in their lives and maybe even lead some of these friends to Jesus. Modeling a missional, outward focus for them is most important to me.

b. That we teach them what the Bible instructs as right from wrong and establish the precepts upon which they will live a victorious life in Christ. It is significantly more important that I fulfill my responsibilities as their parent in this regard than be their friend.

c. That, no matter what, they know I love them and will always be there for them. I will do all I can to care for their needs in good and bad. By doing so, my belief is they know God will always do the same and that they will follow Him faithfully.

d. That they believe in God and in His plan for their lives. I want them to know who God created them to be and to "raise them in the way they should go" by helping them see and believe in their future.

e. That when time comes for them to leave our home, they have all they need to go and accomplish all God has called them to do. Whether we are near or far - in close contact or not - if I have done all I can to make sure this is the case and they do it, then I am fulfilled.

6. My greatest frustration with the church (as a whole) is:
   a. We just don't reach enough people for Jesus. We need to get 'outside the walls' and start reaching those who won't come to church.
   b. We have abandoned spiritual doctrines and Godly instruction. The reason our culture has become so wayward is we have stopped teaching the truth.
   c. There are so many people that fall through the cracks. People come and go without being cared for and remain un-discipled in His love and ways.
   d. We seem to follow the trends of culture rather than setting them. I just know the church could accomplish so much more for Him if we would humble ourselves and take time to ask God to show us what He wants us to do.
   e. We have just stagnated and gotten comfortable with the status quo. There are so many coming to our churches who don't do anything. We need to create more churches, missions, agencies, ventures everywhere in our culture; more opportunities for people to go serve and change the world.

7. I find the following verse most important/inspiring:
   a. 1 Peter 3:15 "Instead, you must worship Christ as Lord of your life. And if someone asks about your hope as a believer, always be ready to explain it."
   b. Joshua 1:8 "Keep this Book of the Law always on your lips; meditate on it day and night, so that you may be careful to do everything written in it. Then you will be prosperous and successful."
   c. Philippians 2:4 "Let each of you look not only to his own interests, but also to the interests of others."
   d. Jeremiah 29:11 "For I know the plans I have for you declares the Lord. Plans to prosper you and not to

harm you. Plans to give you a future and a hope."

e. Luke 10: 1-2 "After this the Lord appointed seventy-two others and sent them on ahead of him, two by two, into every town and place where he himself was about to go. And he said to them, The harvest is plentiful, but the laborers are few. Therefore, pray earnestly to the Lord of the harvest to send out laborers into his harvest."

8. If I could only do one thing for God every day for the rest of my life, it would be:
   a. Verbally share my faith in Jesus with others.
   b. Teach the Bible to all who would listen.
   c. Care for a specific group of people and model the love of Christ to them.
   d. Prayerfully speak God's words and plans over others.
   e. Find great leaders and get them trained and help them obtain what they need in order to do what God wants them to do.

Now, add up the number of checks next to each letter:
   a. _____
   b. _____
   c. _____
   d. _____
   e. _____

The highest total you have corresponds to your potential calling/ core as indicated below:

A- Evangelist; B- Teacher; C- Pastor;
D- Prophet; E- Apostle

If you had a tie between two or more, here's some techniques you can use to help resolve it. Start by asking yourself if you have already experienced instances in which you believe you have functioned more as one calling than another. Your life experience is greatly informative. If that does not help, then ask yourself which calling you would most like to have. Or you can prayerfully decide which one of the above terms most speaks to your heart when you read them. Your holy passions have also been birthed in you by God.

If you still struggle, go back to the exam again and see if there were any scenarios where you really struggled to choose between two possible answers. If choosing the other answer resolves your tie, go with that. And one final way to break a tie might be if one of your top spiritual gifts directly relates to one of the callings. For instance, if you have the gift of prophecy and you are debating between "Prophet" and another. Or if you have the gift of teaching and one of those in debate is "Teacher." If this is the case, you might want to go with that one.

Important to note: many people will grow to have more than one calling at work in your life, though to varying degrees. For instance, you might find the most accurate description for how God uses you to be an 'Apostolic Teacher' or a 'Prophetic Pastor' or what have you. But this comes with significant experience. Even in these cases, those I know who can describe themselves in this way still seem to utilize the one calling as a 'modifier.' In other words, taking the examples I just used, an 'Apostolic Teacher' recognizes their core calling is as a teacher, but they tend to function in an apostolic manner. A 'Prophetic Pastor' would be a pastor at their core, but function in a prophetic manner at times.

The bottom line is, this isn't an exact science. It is really meant to give you a basis or a new direction to consider and use for the rest of the book. You may find the need to refine this more and more. That is good! My hope is this new paradigm of a 'life calling' gives you a revelation of how God wants to use you at some point - whether it is in this moment or a season to come.

Now, this is VERY important! I mean, really, really really….

  …just because you took this test it is not a qualification of any sort of ministerial role. Please don't go around calling yourself 'Evangelist' or 'Apostle' or 'Pastor,' etc. As we said before, there is a difference between a 'calling' and an 'office.' An 'office' is, well, 'official.' An official position could grow out of a calling but it will be confirmed over time (and evidence of fruitful ministry) by other people of God. All of us live on mission, but a 'commission' into a specific ministry is confirmed by both the Holy Spirit and those who love and serve Him.

  A calling is a real thing. You are a gift and it is very likely that you will find the most joy, meaning, and fruitfulness focusing your spiritual gifts in the direction and atmosphere your calling indicates. For instance, if you are an evangelist, you should probably use most of your gifts among people who don't know Jesus. Spending all your time among the saints is probably going to bog you down and make you miserable. Or if you are a pastor, your church life would likely be most fulfilling caring for those who already know Christ.

  We'll talk about this in more detail in the next chapter where we define these callings one by one.

CHAPTER 11

THE CALLINGS – DEFINITION AND FUNCTION

"Are you going to live cautiously or courageously? I called you to live at your best, to pursue righteousness, to sustain a drive toward excellence. It is easier, I know, to be neurotic. It is easier to be parasitic. It is easier to relax in the embracing arms of The Average. Easier, but not better. Easier, but not more significant. Easier, but not more fulfilling. I called you to a life of purpose far beyond what you think yourself capable of living and promised you adequate strength to fulfill your destiny."

Eugene H. Peterson, "Run with the Horses: The Quest for Life at Its Best"[10]

Several years ago, friends of mine were in training to live on mission in Namibia, a small nation that borders South Africa. Many Namibians, even the children, speak at least 4 languages: French, Dutch, English, and Oshiwambo, which is an indigenous language spoken in several African countries. There are actually 13 indigenous languages and dialects spoken in Namibia. As a result of the many languages, my friends had to spend a significant amount of time learning the languages and customs of the people. Typically a missionary may spend a couple of years in these pursuits. The training process for my friends was nearly twice as long. But it was worth it for them to be prepared to head into their new territory - the new place God had prepared for them to live out their calling.

Since you've become more aware of your core calling, you aren't going to head to a new place, necessarily, but, in a spiritual sense, you will be heading into a new 'territory.' (Or it may feel that way for a while.) We are going to spend some time talking about and defining the general nature of the callings. You could spend a great deal of time studying this beyond the definition - years, in fact. We're just going to break the surface here.

The next pages will hopefully bring some clarity to the meaning and function of these core callings. For each calling, I'm providing a simple definition and a short explanation of its root meaning and function. Then, again for each, I will make suggestions on how you might bear fruit in the following arenas of life:

- In a ministry or church body.
- In your career.
- In your family.

The reason I venture into these areas is simple - your

calling involves your whole life and not just one part of it! Or, I guess I could say, your calling represents all of you, not just one part of you. Let's not forget that the supernatural, spiritual aspects of who we are and what we do are the most real of all that is real; as it is the most (and only) permanently enduring dimension of life. As such, it only makes sense that our core as an apostle, prophet, teacher, pastor, or evangelist should impact every aspect of our life, as well as our approach to each arena in which we move. Now, I've never managed a large company and I'm not speaking some of these things out from personal experience. However I have been a student of people's lives over the last 3 decades of ministry, and I am merging some of these experiences with a bit of imagination. I hope they may give you a fresh perspective.

With that said, it's not possible to cover how your specific mix of gifts will influence the ways in which your calling plays out, nor can I imagine every scenario you face. Like so much of this book, this is meant to get your spiritual juices (and, especially, dialogue with God) going.

One final note: while you'll certainly want to focus a bit on the one that matches the results of your quiz, it would be good for you to read through all of them carefully, as the next chapter will deal with how they relate to one another, influence one another, and work together to accomplish the purpose of God's church.

Here's the definitions:

EVANGELIST

The root word from which this calling derives its name means, "to announce news." In the Bible, this phrasing is often translated as, "preach the gospel." The evangelist enacts their passion by specifically compelling those who do not know the Lord to commit their hearts and lives to Him.

While a person who has the calling of an evangelist may very much enjoy church and fellowship with those who know the Lord, they are most likely to have a consistent pull toward those who have not yet heard or do not believe, potentially even finding great ease among people, whether they know the Lord or not. If you have this call, you likely tend to be frustrated when churches prioritize internal events and programs, or allow politics or cultural issues to cloud/inhibit potential relationships with those who do not yet believe. A clear biblical example would be Stephen, the first martyr, who was killed specifically for his uncontainable urge to share his faith and smiled with joy, seeing his death as a reward.

If you tested to be an evangelist in this exam, here's some things to think about:

In church: Look to be involved in or even initiate ministries that emphasize outreach. But don't think you have to wait on anyone. The internet is literally populated by thousands of ways to present the truth of Jesus to those who wish to know about him. Many Bible colleges and seminaries offer free apologetics classes, and you can consider taking one. Start a life group or Bible study in your home and invite your neighbors. There are countless mission agencies that sponsor short-term, evangelistic trips. If your church does, go with them. If they don't, research what's out there, pray about the possibilities, and apply to join them. Trust me, whether it's your neighborhood, your nation, or beyond and into the world, God wants you to go! He's already given all of us permission. And, quite honestly, with your calling, I doubt you're going to be fulfilled until you do.

In your family: Lean in to your natural curiosity and create opportunities that expose your family to new experiences and people. If it applies, some vacation destinations can often serve as great points of outreach. Friends of mine who are absolutely evangelistic would vacation often in Jamaica. They would pack an extra suitcase filled with flip-flops. She would affix tags that said, "Jesus Loves You" and they would take one day and drive out beyond the tourist areas and hand them out to children. At holidays, find ways for your family to serve those in need and share what God has given you.

In your career: As an evangelist, you inherently want to see things get bigger and grow. You are also likely to be keenly interested in maintaining your organization's focus on its core objectives and why it exists. If you are ever given the choice, you are likely to be most fulfilled 'on the front lines' in sales or those aspects of your business that expands clientele. It's not that you can't manage others, but if the responsibilities of overseeing just a few eliminate your ability to develop new relationships, there's a chance you may grow increasingly unsatisfied.

PASTOR

This word derives from the word for 'shepherd.' It literally means, "one who leads to pasture, or sets to grazing, or causes to eat." I believe this definition is really key and helps us latch onto an important distinction you should hold onto if this is your calling. The pastor causes various aspects of discipleship like "eating" (or studying the Bible), gives people the opportunity for exercise of their faith, and makes sure they are growing properly. The pastor doesn't necessarily do all of the teaching or develop the strategies and programs whereby these things take place; but their significant care for a group of people causes them to be certain the right things are happening. A pastor mainly cares that a person is learning Godly character and applying it to their life - not necessarily that they know an extreme level of detail about doctrine. They also want to see the right loving, caring atmosphere among people so a true Godly community can be established. A biblical example is Timothy, who Paul sent in his stead to more deeply establish Godly community in the churches he had planted, and to model the character of Christ as he appointed people to serve.

If you tested to be a pastor in this exam, here's some things to think about:

In church: Quite simple - find a group of people you can care for. This might be a small group or life group, and it can be for any generation or function in the church. You don't even have to lead the group, just be present as a chief influence. Pastors are also attracted to people in need. So, consider care or visitation teams, deacons, or whatever structure your church has for modeling the love of Christ to those who are hurting or challenged in some way. And, this is important, if you see someone who seems down or hurting or alone at church or youth group, go over and talk to them. God has called you to moments like this. There's no reason to wait for someone else to come along. If you're the one who saw them, God is sending you to them.

In your family: You may or may not realize it, but if you aren't married to a person with a pastoral calling, you are likely the atmosphere-setter of your home in many ways, or you have the potential to be. Just as you would with a small group for your church, take responsibility for making sure relationships are healthy and challenges are discussed. Even if you're not given to managing details, try to pitch in on keeping track of doctor's appointments, teacher conferences, etc. Be sure there are enough fun activities to keep people's spirits light. This is really important: practice self care. Be sure you are finding those times to be away from the incessant needs that surround you (even though you care about every one of them!), and be sure some of that time is spent replenishing your own soul.

In your career: If given the opportunity and you aren't already in one, consider a management role. Pastors tend to make great managers. You are attuned to what it takes to setting a positive atmosphere, and you are likely sensitive to people who need help, extra training, or correction/accountability. For some, this may be counter-intuitive. Years ago, a man named Paul volunteered in a youth ministry I oversaw, as a Sunday school teacher. He was one of the most natural pastors I've ever known. The kids learned a lot and they just loved him, and he knew the ins and outs of all of their lives and families.

One day, he mentioned his company was pressuring him to take on a supervisory role, but he was hesitant. He explained his company wasn't the greatest, that he did his job for the paycheck, really, and didn't want more hassle. I reflected to him that I thought he would be great at it. I thought that if he cared about the other guys he worked with like he cared about the kids, that place would never be the same. I honestly didn't think he'd take the suggestion seriously, but a few weeks later he told me he prayed about what I said, and he felt God wanted him to say "yes."

A few months later he called me and thanked me. He said that immediately his boss had allowed him to start to implement changes, and that the employees loved them all. They became more productive, and the company had actually started to be more profitable. He was already given a promotion and significantly more money - all while working less than he did before (which meant he could now volunteer for our Wednesday night youth group!). Best of all, he enjoyed his job for the first time in as long as he could remember.

If you're already a manager, be careful about any advancement that takes you further and further away from a place in which you can demonstrate consistent care over a group of people. Pastors who are promoted into administrative management with decreased interpersonal contact can be at risk of a loss of fulfillment.

TEACHER:

Unlike the other 4 callings, the biblical expression for teacher varies in its context. Throughout the New Testament, it can refer to systematic instruction, to training disciples, to correct or give counsel or simply, to teach. The latter is for general use just as we would in English. It's this general term that is used in Ephesians 4. A teacher, therefore, is really a trainer in God's word, precepts, doctrines, and the whole of His truth in any and all aspects. Whereas a pastor is going to model Christ and see to it that proper training takes place for their disciples, the teacher is the one tasked with doing the actual training itself. Teachers are vital as gatekeepers for sound doctrine, and have a heart for both accuracy and effectiveness. They are driven to research and prayerfully seek understanding. They will think about the best and most effective way to communicate what they have learned so that it sticks. Teachers don't want people to simply hear or know the truths of God, they want them to fully understand these truths, replicate, and be guided by them. A biblical example would be Priscilla and Aquila, who properly instructed and corrected Apollos.

If you tested to be a teacher in this exam, here's some things to think about:

In church: Many of these are obvious opportunities, like leading Bible studies, teaching classes, etc. But, as a teacher, you may find fulfillment instructing anything. Your church likely may have all sorts of systems that guide every team and ministry in your church. Virtually every team needs to have a good teacher to make sure volunteers, or even staff, are trained and ready to do what they are being asked to do. These things can be technical, administrative, best practices, etc. Look for ways you can serve and lead others through teaching even if it isn't strictly teaching the Bible.

In your family: Teach the Bible! You don't need a degree or special classes, you are naturally bent toward finding the correct answers and understanding and then communicating it. So, make the time to lead study of God's word together. Take the lead in helping with homework or coaching for extra activities. Whatever you're doing, think about how you would teach your kids to do it. And, if they're open to it, do so! Even if it only happens every once in a while, as a teacher these moments will become treasured memories.

In your career: Aside from considering a career in teaching (which certainly could make sense) just about every organization and company from small to large, from fast food to bio-technology, needs trainers and teachers of all sorts. In some places, these extra responsibilities may come with little or no extra pay or benefit - but for your own fulfillment, consider doing it and seeing where it leads. Even if there isn't a formal position as such, being seen as the 'go to' person when someone needs to learn the right way to do something can open so many doors for sharing your faith. Think about it - they're already listening to you and have given you some trust. Regardless, you'll likely have more fulfillment from the teaching than the doing.

PROPHET

Standardly, a prophet is defined as a, "proclaimer of God's utterances." A prophet is someone who is going to hear and discern the words of God. Prophets have several consistent desires: they want to share God's deep encouragement with His people; they want every person to know their spiritual calling and gifting; and they want to point everyone toward the future plans He has for each person, the church, and possibly even the world. A New Testament biblical example would be Ananias, who went to Saul (Paul), prayed for him, and spoke the words that God had told him to speak.

If you tested to be a prophet in this exam, here's some things to think about:

In church: Join intercession groups, prayer teams, and seek to be called upon to pray for others. Beyond this, you should truly serve however and wherever you desire to. In whatever atmosphere or whatever team you are a part of, prayerfully seek to be a great encouragement to those around you. Speak God's life-giving words as often as you are prompted to do so, always in submission to whatever leadership is present. As a prophet, the likelihood is high that these moments of sharing are what you will find most fulfilling, even more so than the tasks at hand. As such, a prophet has a great opportunity to be a humble servant, willing to do whatever is needed or asked of you since your ministry function can happen with anyone and at any time. You will also make a great recruiter for whatever team you serve on, as you will likely have insight as to who would be a great fit or is being called by God to serve.

In your family: Study and read the Bible daily, and consider making scripture memorization a priority for you. Pray for and speak words of encouragement over everyone as often as you can. Give your efforts to counseling about the planning of activities, classes, and opportunities for your kids; helping them to discern God's will in all things. Try not to get wrapped up only in your own job and challenges, but think about and pray for your spouse consistently, and if God gives you counsel or direction for them, be sure to share it gently and with love. Either manage or be keenly involved in your family's finances and planning for the future, even if you aren't the most talented or skilled in this area.

In your career: Prophets typically make good entrepreneurs. If you've had an inkling in your heart or mind about starting a business of your own, give it serious consideration. Your ability to envision the future and believe in the good plans of God will serve you well as you get it started. If, however, this is not a desire for you, take a deep and earnest amount of care in the success of whatever company or organization you work for. Ask God to speak to you about its potential and future, and make suggestions from what He shares. Much like in the ministry scenario, you can function within your calling no matter what job you have, and find fulfillment in hearing and sharing the encouragement of God. If you aren't expressly in an HR or recruitment role, you might still find some fulfillment in heading toward a position where you are identifying talent or placing people.

APOSTLE

An apostle literally means, "one who sends." But the definition of the word "send" within that definition can refer to different nuances and abilities. If you have a calling as an apostle, you likely have a little bit of all the other callings mixed into you in various ways. This is because the apostle gets the most spiritual passion by raising up and launching people into what their callings are, and is willing to do whatever they see the need to do, or be whoever they need to be to help them get there. They are the true servant-leaders of the people around them. They want to lead, to initiate, to delegate, and be assured that those around them are properly trained and equipped to do what it is they desire to do for Christ and the world. They typically enjoy creating systems for the accomplishment of this goal. The biblical examples are all of the apostles such as Peter, Paul, Matthew, James, etc...but many like Barnabas lived in that office as well, and it is possible that Lydia may have participated in an apostolic call (if she was key in establishing a church in Thyatira, which is entirely possible.).

If you tested to be an apostle in this exam, here's some things to think about:

In church: Look for opportunities to lead. Based on your spiritual gifts profile, you may enjoy serving and doing things yourself, but God has called you to raise up others to do what you do. When you see a gift in someone, make suggestions on how they can put that into practice. Suggest ideas to your pastoral leadership for new ministry possibilities. If your church has missions ministries or church planting support ministries, strongly consider being involved in these on the conceptual level. You may be used to serving in a particular role because your spiritual gift profile includes an immediate ability to teach or pastor, but you'll find your greatest fulfillment when you are helping others to do ministry. However, the important thing is to look for places in which you are facilitating others using their gifts in some way. You'll maximize the help you can give to your church and discover a new-found joy in how you are serving.

In your family: Initiate the family meetings, Bible studies, devotionals, and step into the role of making sure kids and grandkids are discovering who they are in Christ. You can even do this through church or school activities. You don't necessarily have to be the person who is leading the discussions or taking care of all the details, but you're probably more inclined toward the Godly insight of what your family, and all of its members, really need in order to get to where He wants you to go.

In your career: Look to manage or lead others, particularly when this involves helping others achieve individual accomplishment. Whether this is achieved by starting your own business and employing others or applying for that promotion or opportunity, you'll likely be unfulfilled unless you take that step to oversee and initiate possibilities for other people. You don't need to be a tremendous trainer, but you do have to have a desire to see others trained and perform well. You'll have more joy in what you do in these circumstances, and this joy will make the witness of your faith that much more significant among those with whom you work.

CHAPTER 12

EVERYTHINGIS AWESOME

"It takes two flints to make a fire."

Louisa May Alcott, "Little Women"[11]

As of the writing of this book, if you are under the age of 25 (or have children or grandchildren under that age), when you read the title of this chapter it likely ignited a mental soundtrack of the song by the same title, as performed by the Indie-pop band, 'Tegan and Sara' in 2014 for *The Lego Movie*. And if that happened, you may very well be rather irked at me as the tune's magnificence is that it is equal parts annoying and catchy. In fact, it is so catchy that your temporal lobe either already did move on to play the rest, or is about to sing it out loud as you read this: "Everything is cool when you're a part of a team!"

Now, as you're desperately Googling how to mentally vomit music out of your head for the rest of your day, there is a reason that I did this to the both of us. One of the final lessons of this introduction into spiritual gifts is about how the callings and gifts we have as to the body of Christ relate to one another. Nothing is meant for us to do alone.

God did not desire to live alone. When He created Adam out of the desire for fellowship, the only thing He declared in all of creation as 'not good' was Adam being alone. He even mystically presents Himself as three distinct persons in one rather than being solitary in His very nature. Even when physically present on earth in Jesus, He demonstrated effective ministry by, "sending them out two by two."

The point is, God really likes fellowship and accomplishes tasks by using teams. Anyone who has been around ministry for any length of time knows that this is true. Extremely talented people might be great performers, business people, athletes, and any number of other things entirely on their own; but there are no great isolated Christians or ministers that accomplish much of anything whatsoever without a team around them.

It's not just the fact that we need to have a good team - it needs to be the "right" team, too. For fans of American football, we see this every year. Perennially, there are teams that "win free agency." That is, they go out and spend a lot of money and acquire established superstars to load their roster. Immediately, pundits begin to declare these teams as threats to win the Super Bowl. More often than not, these teams don't win much at all. In some cases, the teams do worse than before the new players arrived. They may have had greater talent, but the talented pieces didn't fit together and function/complement one another as well as they had before.

Over the last 33 years since I have accepted Christ in a Spirit-filled church, I have functioned within, served within, and grown to lead others within the context of spiritual gifts, and the ways God uses us to accomplish His purposes on earth via supernatural means. During this time, I've noticed that various of the five "callings" work in close relationships. Much like Jesus sent out the 72 as I alluded to earlier, these relationships function in pairs.

Certain callings function at their best capacity when they are closely aligned with people of one of the other 4 callings. I have also witnessed how these relationships are specific. If you want to maximize the impact your calling may have on the world around you, I would recommend seeking someone out who has an evident calling like the one that brings out your best potential. If you've been using this book as a group study, then you should take note of whether any of these combinations are present among you. They may become really crucial if you are serving God in the same place at the same time. Let me get right down to my observations, and then I'll unpack it and do a little more explanation.

For instance, I have seen that:

APOSTLES NEED PROPHETS
- Prophets identify the gifts and callings in people that

an apostle is tasked with developing and releasing into the world. Sometimes, apostles are great developers and senders, but they need help seeing and recognizing the specific gifts, abilities, and destinies of the people around them. The prophet can do this.

PROPHETS NEED TEACHERS

- Prophets can get so caught up, at times, in the deeply spiritual revelations that God gives them that they need those who will keep them grounded in accurate, biblical doctrine. Good teachers help prophets keep their imaginations holy and biblically correct. Also and maybe even more obviously, a prophet may stir up a gift or calling in someone but may not be a capable trainer. Therefore, once the gift or calling is identified, the teacher can step in to disciple and prepare them according to what has been revealed.

TEACHERS NEED PASTORS

- Teachers can become so isolated in the pursuit of what is accurate and true that they need those who keep them focused on the hearts, needs, and feelings of the people they are compelled to teach. Pastors help teachers both (at times) soften the blow of hard truths, as well as develop instruction that is applicable.

PASTORS NEED EVANGELISTS

- Pastors can get so consumed with caring for the needs of the people they have been assigned to watch over, they can neglect the great mission we are on to seek and make new disciples. Evangelists inspire pastors to continually expand their perspective to match the heart of God.

EVANGELISTS NEED APOSTLES

- Evangelists will grow dissatisfied with staying inside the church all of the time, but they can also burn out if continuously reaching for harvest in the same location or town with no goal or endpoint. They do best when they are challenged, developed, and sent on assignments to various territories or people. The Apostle is a gift to all, but a treasure to an evangelist.

Just as with much of this book, these observations of mine should be held in the proper context. They are not meant as constraints to who the Holy Spirit wants to pair together. There is so much to human chemistry that can have a tremendous impact on effectiveness. They also are not meant to imply that these are the only relationships that can produce fruit in His kingdom.

However, I do believe these are Spirit inspired revelations that should cause us to think about some things we might take for granted. God has detailed knowledge of who we are and who would make our best co-workers/co-adventurers. Like a loving parent who looks after their child's friendships and is happy when they find a productive match that spurs them on or brings out their best qualities, I think God wants us to be conscious of these possibilities and open to His suggestions as to who might be a good match.

It can be both fun and very useful for us to look more deeply at the relationships we form and why. Leaders and their volunteers/employers and their employees know this extremely well. Literally billions of dollars a year are spent by churches, organizations, and companies of all industries on DISC Profiles, Meyers Briggs, Enneagram, Strengths Finders, etc.

Perhaps, we should put in just a little effort and look to the purely spiritual identities God has given us as we set out to, *"build up the body of Christ until we all reach unity in the faith and in the knowledge of the Son of God and become mature, attaining to the whole measure of the fullness of Christ."* - Ephesians 4:11-14

FOOD FOR THOUGHT
- If reading this with a group, do any of you match up with these pairs of callings? If so, how do you think you could help each other reach your potential? Are you already serving or working together? If so, can you see how you help each other in some of these ways?
- If reading on your own, is there someone you know that you suspect may have the calling that is paired with yours?

CHAPTER 13

HOLY GROUND

"We'll never survive!"
"Nonsense. You're only saying that because no one ever has."

William Goldman, The Princess Bride[12]

So, we've traveled a good bit of ground together, I'd say. In fact, it could be argued we could end here with your gifts and calling all squared away and understood, and call it a day. However, there's one more lesson that I think may benefit you. There's one more encouragement to keep in mind as we come to the end of our journey and I part ways with you. After this, you move on without any need for further guidance from me.

Do you remember the annual 'Presidential Physical Fitness Program' in school? Though it is a voluntary program, nearly all American public schools have participated since President John F. Kennedy instituted it in the early 1960's. So, it's likely most of you reading this do recall it. It's also likely the mention of it brings up a bit of a groan as the memories crystallize. I'm sure there are very few who would say running a mile or doing sit ups and push-ups until you couldn't do them anymore was "fun." This was especially true when your only reward was a super quick rinse off and even more running to get to geometry on time.

I was a decent, but not great, athlete in my school years. I guess you could say I was on the lowest end of 'good' or the highest end of 'average.' So, I wasn't the last guy picked for stuff. I could contribute. When you picked me for your team, you wouldn't be excited, necessarily, but you'd say, "All right, all right, Vinny - cool. Let's go!" And you'd give me a fist bump or high five.

On the PPFP Tests, I pretty much followed this suit. I'd do pretty good to 'okay' at most things. But there was one exercise I absolutely could not do (and still can't.) No matter how I try or how much effort I can conjure - I can't do a single pull-up to save my life. Year after year, I would stretch up as high as I could, hoping the gargantuan Roman nose God gave me would finally serve a useful purpose and lurch above the bar for just a single count of one. Alas, there was never any such fortune. Pull-ups are my absolute bane. The one saving grace about the PPFP throughout my childhood was that boys and girls, for the most part, were evaluated separately. So, when my turn came for the pull-ups, and I was unable to do any of them, I could play it off with a big, "whatever - who cares about this stupid test anyway?" attitude. Some guys might snicker but not with any hostile intent. "Vinny's still cool," they'd mostly, supportively think, and move on to the next guy.

Then, there was a problem. I went to high school. My high school did not have as many bars and apparatuses as my middle school did. So, the girls, who would do something called a "flex arm hang," and the guys, who would do pull-ups had to be tested together - each going up one at a time to the single, metal bar of torture. To make matters even worse, my classmates were trying to make the best of the potential boredom while sitting around and were cheering each other on! But not me. I was in a corner completely silent, sweating and praying my little heart out. I was still a marginal catholic at the time, so I was promising Mary, Joseph, Peter, John, George, Genesius - absolutely any saint I could think of up there - anything that I thought would sound holy enough to compel them to reach down and nudge my rump upward just a couple of times. Or maybe they could create some sort of distraction? Like a fire alarm or an actual earthquake would certainly do. (I wasn't picky.) I just wanted to spare my fourteen-year-old mind the imminent scarring that I was anticipating.

Eventually, the horrible call of my name came up. All of the boys and girls were shouting my name, hooting, and clapping. I said one more quick Act of Contrition and leapt up to grab the bar. I took hold and used all of my might to hoist like I had never hoisted before! My arms were shaking and pumping, my legs were flailing, I was reaching and wrenching my torso as hard as I could from side to side, trying to squeeze another inch higher. I'm sure I must have looked like an infant struggling to be born. I eventually was running out of breath and wheezing, but I just did not want to give in.

After what felt like a half hour, my total was no better than the other 8 or 9 times I had attempted to do this exercise in years past. I failed to do a single one. I dropped down from the bar, dejected. This time, I was unable to muster even a little bit of *laissez faire*, cool, "I don't care" attitude. In fact, my exasperation was met with the very sound that has seared this memory in my mind to this day. No, it was not encouraging cheers. Nor was it deliberate, compassionate statements of exhortation from the coach. Instead, it was absolute, deafening silence.

That's right. No one was saying, "That's all right, Vinny!" or "Next time, Vinny, next time!" Just silence. They weren't even cheering for the next person. Like bystanders of a horrific accident, they were too stupefied to move on from what they had just witnessed. Nearly every single girl I knew was in that gymnasium. They just stared down at the ground, unable to look up. They were likely trying to forget the hideous display of gagging, swinging humanity they had just beheld. Some seemed to be stifling laughter. You could tell the guys were embarrassed for me and were just thanking God it wasn't them.

Now, I could say this made me "scarred for life" but that's not really true. Due to the hyper-speed pace of high school life, it was a topic hushedly shared behind my back for a couple of days, and then another "scandal" had overtaken the rumor mill, and it was forgotten. Truth is, it's funny to me now, and it's kind of fun to share the story with you all these many years after the fact. It was a minor failure. Perhaps you can relate to such an occurrence - a failure that seemed tragic at the time but, in the end, was really a minor event that did not require much healing to overcome.

Not all of our failures are of this variety, right? Each of us has likely encountered days, events, or decisions that have had much farther reaching consequences. There have been major screw-ups. There have been bad decisions. There has been sin. There have been prayers that seemed to go unanswered that spark doubts when you've had a low moment. I think it's important to have a brief discussion and study about these events from our past to be sure we have the proper perspective. The most important thing you need to prepare for now that you have learned your gifts, calling, and purpose, is to act. If past failures or challenges have led to a lack of trust in God or in yourself, you may keep the knowledge you've discovered in this book as just that - knowledge. And knowledge does not transfer into experience until you do something with it.

Let's find some encouragement by looking at a famous episode from the life of Moses. It's the one where he encounters God in a "burning bush." Before we do, let's recount some of Moses' life. You would know these things one of two ways: You either have read them in the book of Exodus 1-3, or you saw the movie *The Prince of Egypt*. Either way, let me recap:

The Hebrew slaves of the Egyptian empire had grown so numerous that Pharaoh had begun to fear they could no longer be dominated and controlled. He issued a decree that all newborn males for a season should be drowned in the Nile. As a result, Moses' family placed him in a basket and floated him down the river. He was found, rescued, and then adopted by the family of Pharaoh, himself!

While there, he was raised in privilege. He received significant education, with most biblical scholars suggesting he may have been an engineer or an architect. Therefore, he created and built and owned things. In fact, he likely shared at least a part of the authority of his adoptive brother and father over everything he could see. However, eventually, as he came nearer to some of the experiences of the Hebrew people he was moved with compassion. God began to change his heart, and he began to realize who he was. He had a deep desire - a calling - that was beginning to form in his spirit that he wanted to help the Hebrews; to deliver them from their plight.

One day, he saw an Egyptian guard beating a Hebrew slave, and he plotted to kill the guard. He looked around to make sure no witnesses were there. Then he ambushed the guard, murdered him, and quickly buried him in the sand.

The next day, he returned to the Hebrew people and saw two of them arguing. He stepped forward to settle the argument and one said, "Who are you? Who made you ruler over us? Or will you kill me like you killed the guard yesterday?"

Moses was taken aback - the body of the guard had been found and Pharaoh was searching for the killer. Moses wasn't alone the night before! He was seen, and it was only a matter of time before his crime was found out. He chose to flee everything - his home and every comfort and privilege - for the cold, lonely wilderness. He eventually found love there with a Cushite woman, and he was accepted into Jethro's family. But, when we catch up to this scene in the book of Exodus chapter 3, he is working as a shepherd - a job Egyptians would have considered detestable for a grown man. They regarded it as something only a child should do. To make things worse, he didn't even own the sheep he was watching over! Moses' failure had caused him to fall from a height of power, influence, and prestige few who lived in any era would know all the way down to this lowly place.

He wasn't quite a slave, but would be considered by most of that time to be not too far from it. This dramatic change of circumstance had exacted a toll on Moses' security and confidence, and it is in this state that we find Moses:

EXODUS 3 - Now Moses was tending the flock of Jethro, his father-in-law, the priest of Midian, and he led the flock to the far side of the wilderness and came to Horeb, the mountain of God. There the angel of the Lord appeared to him in flames of fire from within a bush. Moses saw that though the bush was on fire it did not burn up.

So Moses thought, "I will go over and see this strange sight—why the bush does not burn up." When the Lord saw that he had gone over to look, God called to him from within the bush, "Moses! Moses!" And Moses said, "Here I am." "Do not come any closer," God said. "Take off your sandals, for the place where you are standing is holy ground." Then he said, "I am the God of your father, the God of Abraham, the God of Isaac and the God of Jacob." At this, Moses hid his face, because he was afraid to look at God.

The Lord said, "I have indeed seen the misery of my people in Egypt. I have heard them crying out because of their slave drivers, and I am concerned about their suffering. So I have come down to rescue them from the hand of the Egyptians and to bring them up out of that land into a good and spacious land, a land flowing with milk and honey—the home of the Canaanites, Hittites, Amorites, Perizzites, Hivites and Jebusites. And now the cry of the Israelites has reached me, and I have seen the way the Egyptians are oppressing them. So now, go. I am sending you to Pharaoh to bring my people the Israelites out of Egypt."

But Moses said to God, "Who am I that I should go to Pharaoh and bring the Israelites out of Egypt? And God said, "I will be with you. And this will be the sign to you that it is

I who have sent you: When you have brought the people out
of Egypt, you will worship God on this mountain."

TO SUM UP

- Moses sees God's power on display in an undeniable,
  clear, potent way in a bush that is on fire without burning.
- God tells Moses He has chosen him to go back and finally
  live out the calling that God had placed on his life as a
  deliverer of the Hebrew people which Moses felt when
  he encountered the slave being beaten all those years ago.
- Instead of responding to this invitation with boldness
  and faith, he responds with hesitation born of self-doubt.
  He asks God, "Who am I?"

We might earnestly desire to see God's miraculous
power and to use us as he sees fit. We may even have had experiences where we've seen this kind of outpouring. It takes
a very brief search on YouTube to find countless videos of
worship experiences documenting the miraculous works of
God throughout the world. These episodes would prove that
hundreds of thousands to millions have seen such occur-
rences even in just the last few years. At that rate, you would
expect that, within a short time, nearly every believer would
be able to recount how God had used them in a supernatural
way. And yet, there are more followers of Christ that I know
who couldn't name a single such time, than those who could.

Why is this? I think it may be because many of us have
a tendency to react to the call of God and the compulsion
of the Holy Spirit to step out and use our gifts in the same
way that Moses did. When God prompts us to step out in
faith and pray for a seriously ill or handicapped person, or we
have a compelling need to share an encouraging word with
someone we barely know, or He speaks to us about writing
the book that teaches a new and revealing truth, or perhaps

any other bold act - instead of praying, speaking, writing or doing, we ask Him, "Who am I?"

In that moment, just like Moses, we are allowing the failures and disappointments of our past to keep us from entering into the power and Presence of God. Just like Moses, we remember when others asked us, "Who are you to do _____?" rather than the encouragements of those who love us or of God Himself. We know our past sins and doubts well and think this somehow disqualifies us, or keeps us from being used in greater ways.

Our key to overcoming this is to look at God's answer to Moses' question. God doesn't say to him, "Well, you're the Hebrew I saved from the Nile so that you could be well-educated among the Egyptians, learning all of their customs, perspectives and ways, as well as forming precious relationships in the house of Pharaoh and even with Pharaoh, himself. So, if there was anyone alive with both the capability and knowledge to change Egypt's heart toward my people it would be you." He could have said this. It would have made human sense. But if He had, the focus would have remained on Moses. If He had, then it would have legitimized Moses' doubts because it would indicate the hope of the situation rested on Moses' worthiness and personal strength.

So, that wasn't His answer. He ignored Moses' doubts (because they were irrelevant) and instead, He replied:

"I am with you."

And, if you believe in the word of God and have faith in His promised outpouring of His Spirit, then He is with you, too!

Who was Moses to be the one who would release God's terrible power, and lead and deliver the Hebrews across thousands of miles and decades of time to the brink of their promised inheritance? He was just Moses - the one the Lord was with!

Who are you to be used to bring physical healing, or words of divine wisdom, or teach transforming truths, or lead people higher into their own callings, or raise up and send people into their destinies, or whatever else these tests and assessments have begun to identify and promise for your life?

You are the one God is with.
Full stop. That's all that matters.

Now, you might ask, to what extent does God mean this? I mean, when I sense and feel His presence, then He's with me and He'll use me? When He's not, then I'm off the hook? Let's look again at one key statement from God in the passage. In verse 5, He tells Moses to remove his sandals, "For the place where you are standing is holy ground." Notice, He did not say, "That little patch of sand and dust that you happened to have stumbled upon on your way over I have previously designated as 'holy ground.'"

Again, he said "...the place where you are standing is holy." Why was it holy? The same answer as before - because the Lord was with Moses.

Therefore, wherever Moses went the ground was now holy.
And guess what? The exact same is true for you.

Completely. Absolutely. 100 %. Forever and always, wherever you go - because of your faith in Jesus and the release of the promised Holy Spirit - the Lord is with you. Because He is with you, *wherever* you go is now holy. What does that mean? It means:

Sad places become joyful because *you* are there.
Fearful places become confident because *you* are there.
Chaotic places become peaceful because *you* are there.
Depressed places become encouraging and life-giving
because *you* are there.

The blind see. The lame walk. The sick are made well. Those who despair are lifted up. The lost find their way...because you encounter them! And this is true (and is only true) because of who you bring with you. The Holy Spirit that has irreversibly filled you of His own free will. You couldn't leave Him behind even if you tried! According to the promise of His word, He will never allow anything on, under, or over the earth to separate you from His love, which is His very essence.

He is always with you.

However, none of this is useful if you don't do the one thing I mentioned at the beginning of this chapter: act. This book wasn't meant to deliver a cutesy 'personality type' to talk about with your co-workers for a hot day and a half, hang on your office door, and then forget. If God has revealed anything to you through this book, I pray He has done so in the form of a 150 page call to get back to the most important fundamental:

To exhort you to love others enough to do that which is uncomfortable, unknown, and perhaps even awkward, all while facing down the "Who is he?/Who is she?", and to encourage you to continuously use your faith and your spiritual gifts. In this way, you will supernaturally demonstrate His life-giving power to a lonely and thirsty world.

And if your doubts ever cause you to ask, "Who am I?" Well...
'God is with you, and wherever you go is Holy Ground.'

EPILOGUE

"Roads? Where we're going we don't need roads!"

Dr. Emmet Brown, "Back to the Future"[13]

And so, this brings us to the conclusion of our little stretch of your journey.

I hope we saw some beautiful things together; or, at least, a little out of the ordinary. I hope that some of these things might have caused you to look at God, the world around you, and yourself just a slight bit differently.

Was it, at all, fun? It was meant to be - at least here and there. Not a teasing fun (like it isn't seriously truthful), but the kind of quirky, careless, innocent fun that only people who love God and believe in all He is able to do are afforded the luxury of having.

Above all, I dearly pray this excursion has accomplished what it had set out to do. Namely, that you have a much better, foundational understanding of the nature and purpose of spiritual gifts and, therefore, your nature and purpose in Him as well, and of course, a more specific understanding of your own gifting and calling.

If you were here with me at this moment, it would be my honor to pray with you and prophesy over you; to seek His face and seal His words and His promises to you. In the absence of this, know that my prayers have still been said, and God is absolutely speaking to you even now, and He will never stop.

ONE LAST THOUGHT

C.S. Lewis is often quoted as saying, "I've read the end of the book, and we win!"

Jesus is returning. The same love that powered the creation of the universe, the enduring patience with humanity, the cross, the resurrection, the outpouring of the Holy Spirit, as well as the initiation and fueling of spiritual gifts will see our King return to earth. But there's no reason to just wait patiently.

Once again, I encourage you to take what you have

learned here and demonstrate this love through the supernatural gifts He has given you! Pursue your calling in every aspect of your life and live out the gift He has created you to be for others. Team up with those around you to accomplish the destinies each of you have in your lives, and never stop telling others about the fruit of what He has done. In this way, His return is hastened, and more and more people can look forward to the full "God-magical" instances His supernatural power and the next era of His presence will bring to us all. In other words...

**YOU HAVE SPIRITUAL GIFTS
AND IT'S TIME YOU USE THEM**

REFERENCES

₁Lukas Graham, "Share That Love (feat. G-Eazy)," 2020, Warner Records, Apple Music. Written by Dave Gibson, Digital Farm Animals, Gerald Earl Gillum, Lukas Forchhammer, Morten Ristorp and Neil Ormandy.

₂"The Sporting News" is a trademark of Times Mirror Magazines, New York, NY

₃Condie, Ally. Matched. Penguin Books, 2021.

₄Leake, Jeff, and George Wood. Power For Life: Why Every Believer Needs to Be Baptized in the Holy Spirit. Gospel Publishing House, 2017.

₅U2, "Eleven O'Clock, Tick-Tock", 1980, Windmill Lane Studios, Dublin, Apple Music.

₆Shakespeare, William. Sonnet 116. 2011.

₇Johnson, Bill. Power That Changes the World: Creating Eternal Impact in the Here and Now. Chosen Books, 2015.

₈Spurgeon, Charles. "The Fourfold Treasure," sermon, presented at Metropolitan Tabernacle, April 27, 1871.

₉Lewis, C. The Chronicles of Narnia : The Lion, the Witch and the Wardrobe, Prince Caspian, the Magician's Nephew, the Voyage of the Dawn Treader, the Silver Chair, the Last Battle, and the Horse and the Boy Easton Press 7 Volume Leatherbound Set. Easton Press, 1998.

₁₀Peterson, Eugene. Run with the Horses. Amsterdam, Netherlands, Amsterdam University Press, 2009.

₁₁Alcott, Louisa May. Little Women by Louisa May Alcott. Roberts Brothers, 1868.

₁₂Goldman, William. The Princess Bride: S. Morgenstern's Classic Tale of True Love and High Adventure. Reprint, Harcourt, 2007.

₁₃Zemeckis, Robert, director. Back To The Future. Universal Pictures & Amblin Entertainment. 1985.